YOUR FUTURE IS IN YOUR HAND

DAVID AMOAH

Copyright ©Text 2012 David Amoah and In The Way Publishing© Ltd

The rights of David Amoah to be identified as author of this work have been asserted by him in accordance with the Copyright,

Designs and Patents Acts 1988.

All rights reserved. No part of this publication may be produced, distributed, or transmitted in any form or by any means, including photocopying, recording, or other electronic or mechanical methods, without the prior written permission of the publisher, except in the case of brief quotations embodied in critical reviews and certain other noncommercial uses permitted by copyright law.

For permission requests, write to the publisher, addressed "Attention: Permissions Coordinator" at the email address below:

Life and Success Media Ltd
e-mail: info@lifeandsuccessmedia.com
www.lifeandsuccessmedia.com

Unless otherwise stated, all scripture quotations are taken from the Holy Bible, New King James Version. Quotations marked NKJV are taken from the HOLY BIBLE, NEW KING JAMES VERSION. Copyright © 1973, 1978, 1984 by International Bible Society. Used by permission of Hodder and Stoughton Ltd, a member of the Hodder Headline Plc Group. All rights reserved. "NKJV" is a registered trademark of International Bible Society. UK trademark number 1448790.

Quotations marked KJV are from the Holy Bible, King James Version.

ISBN Number: 978-1-907402-77-7

Dedication

I dedicate this wonderful book to Sister Mary Duah, a member of my church as my appreciation to her for her great contribution towards my first book: 'Lead Us Not Into Temptation'

Contents

Foreword	7
The Purpose And Theme Of This Book:	9
Introduction	17
Foundation Scripture:	19
Examples Of Those Who Used What Was In Their Hand	27
Moses	27
Gideon	33
Abigail	39
The widow's oil	49
The Disciples	59
The Critical Importance Of Using What You Have	63
Seed	71
Knowing and doing your God-given job	74
Protecting your seed	82

Some Of The Reasons Why People Fail To Recognise Or Use What They Have	89
Discouragements from others:	89
Fear:	97
Inferiority complex:	99
Lack of confidence:	102
Laziness:	110
Be The Person God Wants You To Be:	121
Your Availability Will Always Make You Special:	129
The woman of Zarephath	134
Trust and Obey	139
Table Tennis Balls	143
My Testimony	145
Aborted Seeds	149
Conclusion	157
Other Books By The Author	165

Foreword

The future is what you make it, not what someone makes it for you.

He who chooses the beginning of a road also chooses its outcome.

You are what you are and where you are by choice irrespective of your background.

Life is what you make it and from this book you will discover why you must seize opportunities presented to you to engage your gifts and talents i.e. potential to become all you were born to be. YOU CAN MAKE IT. START NOW!

                    -Bishop Michael Hutton-Wood

The Purpose And Theme Of This Book:

✳

The concept of this book, "Your future is in your hand" was born out of a revelation the Lord gave me as I preached a message "What is in your hand?" both in my church and also on my radio program, over a number of weeks. One day as I sat down listening to the recorded version playing on the radio on air, listening and enjoying the power of the message myself, instantly I felt like someone talking to me in the studio, something that occasionally happens to me and I heard the voice of God in the depths of my spirit saying to me, "Do you know your future is in your hand?" Immediately, my own inner voice answered back, "Yes Lord! After all, I've responded to the call of God on my life, I'm a minister, and I'm in the middle of preaching! Is there anything more Lord?" I asked.

Sometime after this experience a fellow minister friend came to see me in my home. As we were talking he picked a book I was reading from my centre table and to my shock and surprise he said "Do you know you can do the same?" I asked him what he meant by that. He said "Do you know that the messages you preach could become books?" "The only thing you need is someone to edit them for you."

When he left I spent time thinking about that short conversation. I also remembered my encounter with the Holy Spirit on the radio the other day so I asked myself 'Could this be the Lord confirming His purpose on my life on top of what I already know?' Later through personal conviction, I settled that this was indeed the leading of the Lord; and that He had something in addition to my work as a pastor that He wanted me to do and that is to convert my preaching into books. So I made a decision to respond to His leading and started to take steps of faith irrespective of how insignificant I felt in the beginning.

The Scripture said, "In all your ways acknowledge him, and he shall direct your paths."
Proverbs 3:6 (NKJV)

The Purpose And Theme Of This Book

As I acknowledged him and asked for His leading, the Lord began to order my steps. He set-up a divine connection and opportunities that led me to write my first book, entitled 'Lead us not into temptation.' The second, 'Be Ye transformed', and this book; "Your future is in your hand."

As an encouragement to you, I have seen clear evidence that, as you begin to use 'what is in your hand' one thing leads to another, and before you know it, you have achieved something you never dreamt was possible. Even though the beginning may be small when you take a step of faith, you'll no doubt see the Lord taking you from glory, to glory all by His Grace. I am also convinced that God gave to every man in his or her hand what he or she will be living on here on earth. Before I move on further let me share my personal testimony with you. As a young man I was educated from Technical School to the Polytechnic where I ended up as a motor vehicle technician. When I finished my education, without getting a job to work with my skills, life wasn't easy, and like so many people I was struggling. I remember during this hard times I decided to use my aunt's old sewing machine to do alterations for people so that could earn me something to live on. One day a very close friend of my father was passing by where I was going on with my business, he stopped, looking at me he said "so after so many years in school, is that what you graduated to do?" It was very embarrassing to hear that but I had to cope with it and therefore said nothing to him. Eventually, although the going was tough, I was later able to set up my own petty trading business until finally in motor vehicle spare parts, and experienced varying degrees of success along the way.

I thank the Lord that after years of working very hard with little real progress, I was called into the ministry and I obeyed the call even though there was a lot of resistance. I am now operating in my calling as a Senior Pastor of The Good Way Apostolic church in London, a preacher, a teacher of God's Word, a radio evangelist and an author. To the praise of His name, I have never been as satisfied with what I am doing as I am now doing what the Lord has called me to do. When I preach on radio listeners are given the chance to call-in as part of the program; some scream over the air in excitement and others speaking in low, convicted, trembling, voices. Often they tell me: how they have been blessed by a message;

how it has changed their lives; how deeply a message has convicted them; and how 'on-point' and personally a topic have been to them. I remember one man who once called and said he was listening to the message from his car radio as he was driving but he has stopped driving because of the conviction of the message and how he is shaking he could not drive so he had to stop. To God be the glory! I have even received calls on several occasions in fact mostly from people who state that they are Muslims who, having been touched by the Word of God, want to hear more about 'this Jesus' I'm preaching about. Some have been ready, then and there to give their lives to Christ! The most fulfilling of the experience I have is when about three listeners have called me and they said to me they were on the point of suicide but having received comfort and encouragement from a message they've just heard, they have regained hope and changed their minds, Hallelujah! I say all this to the glory of God, to make me boast in Him for the gift he has given me; and to encourage you also to discover and use the gifts you have. What could mean more fulfilling than to hear these kinds of testimonies?

The Lord hasn't finished amazing me! When He gave me the message 'Your future is in your Hand?' for preaching (the foundation of this book), like most preachers, little did I realise that the Lord was speaking to me, directly! I came to understand that He wanted me, not just those I was preaching to, to also do something more with my gifts, what he has given me. By His grace and the leading of the Holy spirit, as I said earlier on I'm using what the Lord has given me in another way, and to the Praise of His Name you are reading it now and there is more to come having already written a couple. I'm now using my God-given gifts in diverse ways and have never been as fulfilled, as I am today. I trust that my gift is a blessing to you as you read this book today just as the good Lord intended for me. Also though initially I thought I was writing this book for only believers I discovered later that this life changing piece of information is good for not only believers but for unbelievers too.

As you continue to read, may the Lord, the Most High, who has inspired me to discover even my purpose in my life, help you to discover yours also. Once you've discovered what you also have in your hand, I pray you'll take a leaf out of the book of the biblical characters you'll read about here who, having identified what they had (or had it pointed out to them by someone else!), used it and you will reap the dividend!

✹

Introduction

So many people due to ignorance, fear, lack of faith, sometimes discouragements from others and other factors are weeping out there thinking they have nothing to offer to themselves and to others whilst they sit on the seed of their gifts and talents, or blessing. Others are spending all their time chasing money with less time for God. Others are crying everyday for been poor, praying to God and wondering when they will come out of the financial dungeon not knowing they are sitting on a pot of gold. There are others who also even though may know they have something but put no value on what they've got because it is too small or insignificant. There are others who may not recognise what they have because they think that others do not value it as well. As a result, many turn to fight for what others have whilst others are struggling to trade with things because it is not what has been given to them. I am directed to challenge you with this simple question, **"What is in your hand?"** Recognise what you have, for the gift or talent the Lord have given you is the key to your progress. Even in the house of God people are fighting for positions even though they have not been called into that office and causing a lot of confusion, disunity which also tends to retard the work of the Holy Spirit in that church. I believe it is most important and imperative for everyone to discover what the Lord has given them. I also believe that most failures in life are due to the fact many have failed to discover this fact which is God's purpose in their lives. Based on Exodus 4:1-4 the foundational Scripture of this book I want to challenge you to know what you have in your hand, your gift and talent, God's purpose for your life and then begin to work with it and the Lord will bless you for that is your future.

✻

Foundation Scripture:

✳

The entire account of Moses, God's people (Israel) fleeing Egypt and the parting of the Red Sea in the Book of Exodus gives us divine insight into the importance of using what we have or indeed what we have been given to 'deliver' our lives and those of others. Exodus 4:2 specifically provides the symbolic reference, the scriptural foundation and the title for this book. After the Lord had spoken to Moses in Exodus 3 about delivering His people from the hand of Pharoah, we read in Exodus 4:1-4:

"And Moses answered and said, But, behold, they will not believe me, nor hearken unto my voice: for they will say, The LORD hath not appeared unto thee. And the LORD said unto him, What is that in thine hand? And he said, a rod. And he said, Cast it on the ground. And he cast it on the ground, and it became a serpent; and Moses fled from before it. And the LORD said unto Moses, put forth thine hand, and take it by the tail. And he put forth his hand, and caught it, and it became a rod in his hand."

The full account of this narrative begins in Exodus 3:7-11, when the Lord speaks to Moses in the burning bush.

"And the LORD said, I have surely seen the affliction of my people which are in Egypt, and have heard their cry by reason of their taskmasters; for I know their sorrows; and I am come down to deliver them out of the hand of the Egyptians, and to bring them up out of that land unto a good land and a large, unto a land flowing with milk and honey; unto the place of the Canaanites, and the Hittites, and the Amorites, and the Perizzites, and the Hivites and the Jebusites. Now therefore, behold, the cry of the children of Israel is come unto me: and I have also seen the oppression wherewith the Egyptians oppress them. Come now therefore, and I will send thee unto Pharaoh, that thou mayest bring forth my people the children of Israel out of Egypt."

Remember, scripture says here,

"And the LORD said ... I am come down to deliver them out of the hand of the Egyptians" Yet, it is important to note also that in verse 10 He says to Moses: '... Come now therefore, and I will send thee unto Pharaoh, that thou mayest bring forth my people the children of Israel out of Egypt."

There is a critical lesson here about the use of our gifts. The 'plan' and the 'purpose' are God's, His divine will; but He uses us, man empowered with His abilities, to fulfil His divine will!

Exodus, chapter 3 also begins the series of events and miracles that result in Israel's deliverance from Egypt's Pharoah, his people and his army. The first series of events and miracles is the removal of the first set of obstacles. Namely: Moses' reluctance at being called by God to deliver His people; Moses' awareness of his own weaknesses; and Moses' fear of the might and power of Pharaoh and his army. When we read on from Exodus 3:8-21 through to Exodus 4:17, we see that despite God's instruction 'Come now therefore, and I will send thee'; and His constant step-by-step instructions and reassurances to Moses – Moses persists in questioning God, raising objections and making excuses.

In fact, Moses manages to raise seven separate reasons why he was not the right man for the job; and therefore wouldn't be able to obey God.

When you read the scriptures for yourself you'll find Moses said:

1. "Who am I, that I should go unto Pharaoh, and that I should bring forth the children of Israel out of Egypt?" (Exodus 3:11, KJV)
2. "Suppose I go to the Israelites and say to them, 'The God of your fathers has sent me to you,' and they ask me, 'What is his name?' Then what shall I tell them?" (Exodus 3:13)
3. "But behold, they will not believe me ..." (Exodus 4:1, KJV)
4. "... nor hearken unto my voice: for they will say, The LORD hath not appeared unto thee." (Exodus 4:1, KJV)
5. "... O Lord, I have never been eloquent, neither in the past nor since you have spoken to your servant ..." (Exodus 4:10)

6. "... but I am slow of speech and of tongue." (Exodus 4:10, KJV), and
7. "O Lord, please send someone else to do it." (Exodus 4:13) Moses persisted in his self-justification until the Bible says in Exodus 4:14: "... the anger of the Lord was kindled against Moses", KJV

It is agreed by Biblical scholars that Moses himself was naturally prone to anger and impatience. I'm not saying that consequently he must have been angry or impatient with God nor am I saying that this must have been the reason why he made excuses; and in the end exasperated the Lord when he requested He 'send someone else'. But, it's an interesting thought!

What is true is that Moses was a man just like us, and we like him all have character flaws! Could your disposition or attitude be the reason why you're not operating in your gifts and talents? We'll take a look at this issue more closely later under the heading 'Why Some Christians don't operate in their giftings.'

But for now, take note that five out of the seven objections Moses raised were self-justifications or self-condemnations. This shows that the overwhelming majority of his reasons, about 70%, were about himself and what he saw as his inadequacies while, just under 30% of his reasons were about what he believed to be the opinion of others. This shows that Moses was just like the majority of us who put ourselves down and magnify the opinions of others! Moses had no confidence in himself even though the Lord had other views of him. Think about it!

Suffice to say here, that if we are presently not operating with 'what we have in our hands'; then like Moses we may be making excuses about our real or imagined inadequacies. Or, it may be like Moses we are dwelling on the possible negative opinions others may have about us.

If so, I would respectfully suggest that we ourselves have become obstacles to our progress!

It means that just like Moses, even before we've left the starting block, we've concluded the matter in our hearts and minds with negative thoughts and by our mouths, with negative confessions. I've known of people talking themselves out of jobs that they could do and would probably be successful at securing. Yet, they disqualified themselves in their hearts and minds; so much so that they never even attempted to be interviewed! People in this kind of situation make 'Moses-like' excuses – 'I'm not good enough', 'I'm not skilled or experienced enough', 'people won't like me', 'they'll never give me the job', 'I don't have the right accent ', 'I'm not the right race, or gender, or size, or age', 'I don't have a good enough education', 'I can't. These are all reasons people cite for not trying, just like Moses.

When Moses made excuses, the Lord asked him a specific question: 'What is that in your hand?' (Exodus 4:2, KJV)

The question is, why didn't Moses focus on what the Lord was asking? Was it that Moses did not value the 'rod' in his hand that the Lord was drawing his attention to? Was it that he had no confidence in himself or his ability to perform the task God was calling him to? Could it be that his fears so blinded him, he voiced objections which seemed to doubt God? But, Hallelujah! we can take comfort from the fact that despite all of Moses' excuses (and our own), He who knows the end of a matter before the beginning of it is still omniscient (all knowing)! The Lord insisted that Moses was the 'one'.

Even though Moses seemed to have written himself off completely and 'angered' the Lord as well, the Lord hadn't and didn't give up on Moses. Instead, our merciful and compassionate Lord said: "Now go; I will help you speak and will teach you what to say" in Exodus 4:12. Likewise the Lord has not given up on you. You have something in your hand too. If you are willing and obedient, the Good Lord Himself will lovingly help and direct you in what you have. He'll even guide, help and teach you how to use it. But, you must first make up your mind and agree in your heart to work with Him!

✺

Examples Of Those Who Used What Was In Their Hand

Moses (Exodus 3 & 4)

From the previous chapter, 'What is in Your Hand?' we saw that Moses was not enthusiastic when commanded by God to get His people out of Egypt. We read about the seven reasons Moses gave to explain why he couldn't/shouldn't follow the direct instruction from the Lord – 'come now therefore, and I will send you' in Exodus 3:11, KJV. We noted that the majority of Moses' objections were self-condemnations – him writing himself off.

As the Bible says in Matthew 12:34:

> "... for out of the abundance of the heart the mouth speaks."

It raises the question 'What was in Moses' heart when he said what he said to God?' More to the point, what are you saying in your heart about yourself? While you consider the question, let's look a little deeper into the life of Moses to see something interesting. Biblical scholars agree that for the benefit of study and analysis Moses' life can be divided into three, forty year periods.

The first forty year period was from his childhood to his exile from Egypt. Moses was born at a perilous time to Israelite parents, when Israel was enslaved to the Egyptians. At the time there was a royal edict, ordering the execution of all Israelite male children. Moses was hidden among the reeds by the river bank, by his mother and sister Miriam and drawn from the Nile by Pharaoh's daughter. Adopted by her, Pharaoh's daughter raised Moses as her son. So, Moses was groomed and trained in the grand courts of Egypt, as a royal prince. Here Moses became "learned in all the wisdom of the Egyptians and was mighty in words and in deeds" as stated in Acts 7:22.

His training in Egypt would later qualify Moses to write the *'Pentateuch'* the five books of the Hebrew *'Tôrâh'*, (meaning direction or guidance from God), the first five books of the Old Testament namely: Genesis, Exodus, Leviticus, Numbers and Deuteronomy. During this first forty year phase of his life, Moses would have known: the Egyptian, Babylonian and Hebrew languages; Hebrew and Babylonian classics; civil administration and military science. He led a wealthy life as would have been fitting for a future pharaoh. He doubtless would have been a powerful man in the royal court, with plenty of servants at his beck and call.

Following his flight from Egypt to Midian, Moses lived the next forty years, the second period of his life, like a nomad of the day in the parched desert herding flocks. He chooses to turn his back on the life and kingly destiny in Egypt. The writer of the book of Hebrew said "By faith Moses, when he became of age, refused to be called the son of Pharaoh's daughter, choosing rather to suffer affliction with the people of God than to enjoy the passing pleasures of sin, esteeming the reproach of Christ greater riches than the treasures in Egypt; for he looked to the reward. By faith he forsook Egypt, not fearing the wrath of the king; for he endured as seeing Him who is invisible". Hebrews 11:24-27 (NKJV)

It is in Midian that he meets and marries Zipporah, daughter of the wise and pious Jethro and tended Jethro's flock. Over these forty years he would certainly have become very familiar with lonely, nomadic, desert life – a life roaming in the wilderness! The final forty year period of Moses' life starts from the exodus of Israel from Egypt, to his death on Mount Nebo. It stands to reason that when he was in the courts of Pharaoh, and during the forty years he spent in the desert in the wilderness; the Lord must have been preparing Moses for His purposes, which occupied the last forty years of Moses' life. Moses' destiny was to be an instrument of deliverance for God's people, Israel. Exodus 3:1 says: "Now Moses kept the flock of Jethro his father in law, the priest of Midian and he led the flock to the backside of the desert, and came to the mountain of God, even to Horeb."

Moses had long-term experience of 'keeping' something for another – 40 years experience in fact. *'He kept the flock of Jethro his father in law.'* He had experience of 'leading' a multitude of sorts – *'he led Jethro's flock'*;

and he had experience of leading through the wilderness – *'he led the flock to the backside of the desert and came to the mountain of God, even to Horeb'*.

It is interesting to note here that throughout the Old Testament the word 'flock' is often used to refer to Israel as" sheep" gathered by God, the Lord being their Shepherd! So, Moses 'kept', he 'led', and had 'wilderness experience'. Moses had a track record. He had what are called today 'directly, transferrable skills'. His leadership skills, organisational skills, knowledge of geography, knowledge of the history of Israel, knowledge of the desert, writing skills and skill in oral traditions, were all critical to his eventual destiny. His total 'know-how' enabled him to lead Israel through the wilderness and leave a lasting legacy. Clearly, Moses also had an astonishing relationship with the Almighty. This is particularly seen in his desire to ensure that Israel in order to continue to enjoy the favour of God unto generations should be careful to conform to the 'law'; which emerged divinely from the Lord, during the wilderness years.

Certainly, Moses' 'wilderness skills' must have come in handy and he used them to great effect when he 'led' Israel, God's people and others, out of Egypt and through the desert.

With all this amount of skill and knowledge, it still begs the question, why was Moses so hesitant in the beginning? Could his reluctance be because he undervalued his abilities; couldn't 'see' what he had which is why the Lord had to ask him the question, to prompt Moses to 'see'?

Does this sound familiar? Like Moses are you reluctant to use what you have or are you guilty of blindness about the skills you possess; your years of experience or the opportunities presented to you? Your experience (work-related, voluntary, in the home, and of life) and what you know how to do and do well are all elements of your abilities and talents. What experience do you have? What do you know how to do and do well that you could be using to the benefit of your church, others and yourself to the glory of God? Think about it!

With the instruction, encouragement and presence of the Lord, as he used 'what was in his hand', Moses went on to become known as the 'Father' of the nation of Israel; their deliverer; the 'law-giver', the one who prepared Israel to enter Canaan.

Gideon (Judges 6:12-17)

The account of Gideon and his total ignorance and lack of confidence in what he had, should be a sobering lesson to us all.

Gideon was the fifth of the twelve judges of Israel, the 'twelve military rulers', whom the Lord raised up to deliver Israel "out of the hand of those who spoiled them." (Judges 2:16b)

We find the backdrop to the accounts of the twelve judges of Israel, including Gideon, in the following scriptures:

1. Judges 17:6 – "In those days Israel had no king; everyone did as he saw fit."
   (see also Judges 18:1, Judges 19:1 and Judges 21:25)
2. Judges 2:11 – "Then the Israelites did evil in the eyes of the LORD and served the Baals."
3. Judges 2:14 – "And the anger of the LORD was hot against Israel, and he delivered them into the hands of spoilers

that spoiled them, and he sold them into the hands of their enemies round about, so that they could not any longer stand before their enemies." NKJV, and

4. Judges 2:16 – "Nevertheless, the LORD raised up judges who delivered them out of the hand of those who plundered them." NKJV

The work and accomplishments in the years of oppression and peace of the four Judges before Gideon, covers some 200 years. Yet, after the death of the fourth Judge, Barak who was helped during his term by the only female Judge Deborah (see Judges 4-5), Israel returned to its idolatrous ways. So, the anger of the Lord was once again against Israel and He delivered them into the hands of the Midianites for seven years (see Judges 6:2-6). As a result:

> "... Israel was greatly impoverished because of the Midianites; and the children of Israel cried to the LORD. And it came to pass, when the children of Israel cried to the LORD because of the Midianites, That the LORD sent a prophet to the children of Israel, which said to them, Thus said the LORD God of Israel, I brought you up from Egypt, and brought you forth out of the house

of bondage; And I delivered you out of the hand of the Egyptians, and out of the hand of all that oppressed you, and drove them out from before you, and gave you their land; And I said to you, I am the LORD your God; fear not the gods of the Amorites, in whose land you dwell: but you have not obeyed my voice. And there came an angel of the LORD, and sat under an oak which was in Ophrah, that pertained to Joash the Abiezrite: and his son Gideon threshed wheat by the wine press, to hide it from the Midianites." - Judges 6:6-11, NKJV

Fearing the prophet's prediction, Israel once again repents and cries out to the Lord. This is where we are introduced to Gideon when the angel of the Lord appears to him:

"The angel of the LORD came and sat down under the oak in Ophrah that belonged to Joash the Abiezrite, where his son Gideon was threshing wheat in a winepress to keep it from the Midianites." (Judges 6:11)

Whereupon, the angel commissions him to take command of the forces of Israel:

> "The Lord is with you, you mighty man of valour!" Gideon said to Him, "O my lord, if the Lord is with us, why then has all this happened to us? And where are all His miracles which our fathers told us about, saying, 'Did not the Lord bring us up from Egypt?' But now the Lord has forsaken us and delivered us into the hands of the Midianites." Then the Lord turned to him and said, "Go in this might of yours, and you shall save Israel from the hand of the Midianites. Have I not sent you?" So he said to Him, "O my Lord, how can I save Israel? Indeed my clan is the weakest in Manasseh, and I am the least in my father's house." And the Lord said to him, "Surely I will be with you, and you shall defeat the Midianites as one man." Then he said to Him, "If now I have found favour in Your sight, then show me a sign that it is You who talk with me." - Judges 6:12-17, NKJV

There is a deep revelation here that I want you to get hold of!

Take note that Gideon is threshing wheat by hand, not having his servants do it with oxen which would usually have been the case.

He definitely had servants that could have threshed the wheat for him *(see Judges 6:27)*. But, he was actually threshing wheat himself with a staff.

When the angel tells Gideon in Judges 6: to: "Go in this might of yours', I believe he is saying two things. (1) Go and use this 'I can do' spirit you have, for the higher purpose of God, and (2) Go in the expectation that the Lord is supposed to and will be with you. I am right to say, He the angel of the Lord, realised that Gideon could use the same humility, strength, commitment to purpose and expectation of the Lord's presence, to *'thresh'* (beat) the Midianites for the Lord.

Unfortunately, just like most of us, Gideon had no regard for what he had in his hand, and what it could be used for. Just as we are often not encouraged by a word from the Lord or from those around us, who believe in and acknowledge our abilities, Gideon was not encouraged by the prophetic words of the angel *'mighty man of valour'*.

Like Moses, and just as we do, Gideon gave so many objections and reasons why he was the wrong man and the circumstances were wrong! He had faith and expectation, but felt Israel had been forsaken. So, he clung desperately to the angel's assurance that he would have the presence of God and asked for a sign to confirm that he was actually in the company of the Lord. Let me say here that there is nothing wrong with wanting assurance of God and waiting for his leading, it is actually an act of faith. But there's a point at which you have to also take a step of faith, take some action. Remember faith without works or a corresponding action is dead faith! *(James 2:26)*

What I love about the Lord is that even the sign He gives to Gideon when Gideon asks for one, was meant to remind Gideon that he needed to use what *he had* in his hand just as the angel used what was in his – Praise His name! "With the tip of the staff that was in his hand, the angel of the LORD touched the meat and the unleavened bread. Fire flared from the rock, consuming the meat and the bread. And the angel of the LORD disappeared. When Gideon realized that it was the angel of the LORD, he exclaimed,

"Ah, Sovereign LORD! I have seen the angel of the LORD face to face!" But the LORD said to him, "Peace! Do not be afraid. You are not going to die." So Gideon built an altar to the LORD there and called it The LORD is Peace. To this day it stands in Ophrah of the Abiezrites." (Judges 6:21-24)

Do you have faith, but feel as though God has been waiting for you to make a move or 'get right' with Him for so long, that He has given up on you? Let me assure you, once you are His, He hasn't and He won't. Remember He has promised never to leave nor forsake you *(1 Kings 8:57)*. Repent of your sin and your doubts if you are guilty and you've been habouring doubt, then step out in faith!

Abigail

The account of Abigail is a stunning example of someone using what they have, to better their situation and the lives of others.

The Bible tells us in 1 Samuel 25:3 that Abigail, the wife of the very rich but bad-mannered and evil Nabal, was an intelligent and beautiful woman. Unlike her uncivilised husband Nabal who didn't have the character typical of men of his particular line, Abigail displayed wisdom, tact, generosity and humility. Nabal was actually of the Tribe of Judah, the same tribe as David. As we'll see, ultimately Abigail used all her various gifts (what she had in her hand!) to avert major bloodshed, safeguard the kingly destiny of David and protect her current and future households. From 1 Samuel 25:4-8 we learn that David heard Nabal was conducting a sheep-shearing festival. An ancient custom and traditionally a time of hospitality and generosity on the part of sheep masters, like Nabal.

David was aware that the presence and reputation of his 600 strong, battle-hardened, army of raiders in the wilderness of Carmel, had protected Nabal's flocks (three thousand sheep and a thousand goats) and his shepherds. In fact, the Bible says Nabal's flock and shepherds were 'with' David's men, which means they were effectively 'covered' by David's men. Even Nabal's servants later said of David's men to Abigail in 1 Samuel 25:15-16:

> "Yet these men were very good to us. They did not mistreat us, and the whole time we were out in the fields near them nothing was missing. Night and day they were a wall around us all the time we were herding our sheep near them."

So David sent a delegation of ten men to Nabal and told them to greet Nabal in his name and in peace; and ask for a token of his abundance. Apparently, the size of the delegation David sent would have been a sign to Nabal of the respect David had for him. David explicitly told his men to let Nabal know that they hadn't harmed Nabal's men or sheep; nor stolen from them (which implies that they could have!).

Given our theme, note what David respectfully says in 1 Samuel 25:8:

> "Ask your young men, and they will tell you. Therefore let my young men find favour in your eyes, for we come on a feast day. Please give whatever comes to your hand to your servants and to your son David." NKJV

Give *"whatever comes to your hand to your servants, and to your son David"*. What did Nabal have in his hand? He had wealth and flocks, but he also had in his hand – within his power – the ability and the opportunity to show appreciation to his 'son David' (that is his kinsman from same Tribe of Judah) and David's men.

Clearly, David felt that his men had 'served' Nabal, and served him well in protecting his wealth. He respectfully calls his own men Nabal's servants! I believe that David probably hadn't allowed his men to raid Nabal, because he recognised and respected their shared kinship.

David assumed that, as was the custom, Nabal would appreciate the service his men had rendered and that Nabal would honour the 'debt' to him with 'tribute', that is some of the food and wine being enjoyed at the festival. This is because 'tribute' would usually be given in these circumstances and at this time ('in a good day' during the shearing festival when there was abundance and celebration), with good will and gratitude. As was the practice of the day, if 'tribute' was not given freely by the sheep masters, it could be enforced as a right.

In his response to David's men who faithfully delivered David's message to Nabal, Nabal comments in 1 Samuel 25:9-11

'Who is this David, who is this son of Jesse?' and *'many servants are breaking away from their masters'* reveal Nabal's foolhardy character and the fact that he knew of David, but pretended he didn't. Nabal could have played things very differently! He must have heard of David's exploits, and the fact that he was anointed to be King of Israel one day. By refusing to give David's men anything, Nabal effectively didn't maximise the opportunity he had in his hand! It's a lesson to us all. Not using what you have in your hand, what opportunity could you be missing? What disasters could you be averting when you do use your gifts and opportunities?

In fact, Nabal's refusal was actually against custom and an insult to David and his men who went back to David with Nabal's answer to his request. 1 Samuel 25:13, 22 tells us exactly the result of Nabal not using 'what he had in his hand':

> "David said to his men, "Put on your swords!" So they put on their swords, and David put on his. About four hundred men went up with David, while two hundred stayed with the supplies." In 1 Samuel 25:13 and 22 David says: "May God deal with David, [a] be it ever so severely, if by morning I leave alive one male of all who belong to him!"

It's at this point that Abigail, the focus of our investigation, is spoken of. It is worth mentioning here that Nabal's men who overheard Nabal talking to David's men, didn't speak to or advise Nabal. They knew he was an unreasonable and worthless man (a son of Belial), as we'll see in a moment. So, it would have been pointless speaking to him. "One of the servants told Nabal's wife Abigail:

> "David sent messengers from the desert to give our master his greetings, but he hurled insults at them." (1 Samuel 25:14, 17) "Now think it over and see what you can do, because disaster is hanging over our master and his whole household. He is such a wicked man that no one can talk to him."

Clearly, Nabal's men knew Abigail was an intelligent woman who could and would do something rather than let them all be killed!

As we'll see in the King James Version of 1 Samuel 25:18 below, *'Abigail made haste'*. She didn't waste time and she didn't have to contemplate on what she would do for hours, days, months, years, before taking action! Because Abigail had the skill and the opportunity to do so, she acted immediately. She didn't even tell her husband what she was going to do! That fact is another message entirely and one I'm not about to treat here!

I want you to picture something else! 1 Samuel 25:18-19 says:

> "Then Abigail made haste, and took two hundred loaves, and two bottles of wine, and five sheep ready dressed, and five measures of parched corn, and an hundred clusters of raisins, and two hundred cakes of figs, and laid them on asses. And she said unto her servants, Go on before me; behold, I come after you. But she told not her husband Nabal." KJV

Abigail used her hospitality gifts, wisdom gifts and the advantage of an impressive caravan of asses, loaded down with food for David's men to create a positive impression and maximise an opportunity. Not only that, the five sheep were *'ready dressed'* which meant that all David's hungry men had to do was roast them! Abigail thought of everything! The account goes on to tell us that she followed the caravan of asses and when she saw David:

> "... she hasted, and lighted off the ass, and fell before David on her face, and bowed herself to the ground, And fell at his feet, and said, Upon me, my lord, upon me let this iniquity be: and let thine handmaid, I pray thee, speak in thine audience, and hear the words of thine handmaid." - 1 Samuel 25:23-24, KJV

By prostrating, face down on the ground, at his feet, Abigail humbled herself before the future King of Israel. Although the insult had come directly from her husband, she took total responsibility for 'this iniquity' saying in 1 Samuel 25:25c: "... as for me, your servant, I did not see the men my master sent." and in 1 Samuel 25:28,

> "Please forgive your servant's offense, for the LORD will certainly make a lasting dynasty for my master, because he fights the Lord's battles. Let no wrongdoing be found in you as long as you live."

She addressed herself as David's servant. Clearly, she was implying that it was her fault entirely, as it was her duty to serve David her *'master'* the anointed of God, and his men.

Abigail's speech that follows from 1 Samuel 25:24-32, is the longest speech by a woman in the Bible. Her assessment of the situation that it was the Lord who had kept David from avenging himself with his own hand by bringing her to him, her pointing out the jeopardy David would unnecessarily put his destiny in if he were to shed the blood of Nabal and his men and her recognition of and concern for David's destiny, all moved him to grant her request. David said to Abigail:

> "May you be blessed for your good judgment and for keeping me from bloodshed this day and from avenging myself with my own hands. Otherwise, as surely as the LORD, the God

> of Israel, lives, who has kept me from harming
> you, if you had not come quickly to meet me,
> not one male belonging to Nabal would have
> been left alive by daybreak."
> (1 Samuel 25:33-34)

Abigail had prevented David from taking the law into his own hands. She had prevented him from using 'what was in his hand' – his right to vengeance, and presented what was in her hand – a divine solution to a major crisis! Hallelujah!

"Then David accepted from her hand what she had brought him and said,

> "Go home in peace. I have heard your words
> and granted your request." (1 Samuel 25:35)

What gift do you have and how do you use it? Do you use your intelligence, beauty or looks to promote godliness; and to bring about peace or have you put your 'confidence' in your flesh? Some people use their gifts, talents and positions to encourage, help and support their partners, whilst others don't at all. But, like Abigail who used her gift wisely, choose to use yours wisely for God, your household, and church. Like Abigail, as a consequence, not as the purpose of it, you too will receive a reward.

Just ten days after Nabal's death, David married Abigail. I believe David was not about to let such a choice woman get away! Through the next biblical account we see the truth at work that, God multiplies what we surrender to him.

The widow's oil (2 Kings 4:1-7)

"A certain woman of the wives of the sons of the prophets cried out to Elisha, saying, "Your servant my husband is dead, and you know that your servant feared the LORD. And the creditor is coming to take my two sons to be his slaves." So Elisha said to her, "What shall I do for you? Tell me, what do you have in the house?" And she said, "Your maidservant has nothing in the house but a jar of oil. Then he said, "Go, borrow vessels from everywhere, from all your neighbours' empty vessels; do not gather just a few. And when you have come in, you shall shut the door behind you and your sons; then pour it into all those vessels, and set aside the full ones." So she went from him and shut the door behind her and her sons, who brought *the vessels* to her;

and she poured *it* out. Now it came to pass, when the vessels were full, that she said to her son, "Bring me another vessel." And he said to her, "*There is* not another vessel." So the oil ceased. Then she came and told the man of God. And he said, "Go, sell the oil and pay your debt; and you *and* your sons live on the rest."

The above story of the account of the widow and Elisha's miracle in multiplying what she had (the small oil), is a lesson to everybody especially all those who may have the opportunity to read this book in our willingness to use what little we have to improve our lot and that of others. She also demonstrated faith, trust, and obedience in action. The Scripture says that her husband is dead, her two sons; her hope for the future, were in danger of being taken away by her creditor to be his slaves. But what this widow did not know was that she was sitting on a 'pot of gold', something that could lift her from her financial bondage. Many people like the widow woman are overwhelmed with mounting debts, lack of a job and no clear way through their financial problems. Yet, they could be sitting on the very means, the

God-given gifts and talents that could bring them financial independence.

The widow believed she could do nothing about her situation herself, but she knew that the man of God could. She knew that the man of God could do something, even though she did not know exactly what he will do but she had an expectation for the sake of her husband who had served the prophets, including him faithfully – remember she said to Elisha 'your servant, my husband is dead'. From the account, we see that Elisha was indeed able to help her, but she had to do something. She had a part to play in her own liberation from her troubles.

> "Elisha replied, "How can I help you? Tell me, what do you have in your house?" In the context of the theme of this book, Elisha asked her 'what is in your hand' "Your servant has nothing there at all," she said, "except a little oil." (2 Kings 4:2) In other words, she said 'I have nothing in my hand "except a little oil."'

What the widow didn't know was that what she had was a seed. Something if it is given out or put into use God could be turned into something big. She didn't realise that in her position of lack and desperation, she still had something that could be surrendered, for the prophet to do something with it. What do you have that you could render to the Lord and see the truth in action as the Lord multiplies it? This is what Elisha did for the woman and her sons when she obeyed his instructions. In 2 Kings 4:3-7 we read:

> "Elisha said, "Go around and ask all your neighbours for empty jars. Don't ask for just a few. Then go inside and shut the door behind you and your sons. Pour oil into all the jars, and as each is filled, put it to one side." She left him and afterward shut the door behind her and her sons. They brought the jars to her and she kept pouring. When all the jars were full, she said to her son, "Bring me another one." But he replied, "There is not a jar left." Then the oil stopped flowing. She went and told the man of God, and he said, "Go, sell the oil and pay your debts. You and your sons can live on what is left."

We see from the story that the woman acted upon the instructions of the prophet, went out to borrow as much jars she could get, shut the door and began to pour the oil into them one after the other until there were no more jars left. Reporting to the prophet he said

"Go, sell the oil and pay your debts. You and your sons can live on what is left."

This means the woman became debt-free that day and had extra money to buy food to eat with the oil.

Besides this I had two revelations about this woman's encounter with the man of God, which I'd like to share with you.

First! How much consideration have you given to the idea of speaking to your Pastor, about your aspirations? How many times have you spoken to him or her about your plans or what you'd really like to do for a living? When did you speak to your Pastor about how well things are going for you in your business? People only seem to go to their Pastors who are supposed to be their spiritual fathers and mothers only when they're already in trouble or there is a problem. I'm not saying that people shouldn't go to their Pastors for help in difficult times, in fact they most definitely should. What I am saying is that many people think making known to his or her pastor what he or she has or does for living or telling them about how things are going with them will allow the pastor to make demands from them so they hide from them what they have or do and will only go to them when they are in trouble. What people don't know is sharing your heart with your pastor about what you have or do as well as your problem will enable him or her to remember you always in his or her prayers.

If you have a gift or talent and you want to step out in faith to do something with it inside or outside your church don't be reluctant to go to your Pastor or the minister responsible for these matters in your church, for guidance. Don't only tell your Pastor your problem and ask for prayers but also be willing to share with him or her also when things are going well when the Lord blesses you.

Secondly! For the prophet to tell the woman "Go around and ask all your neighbours for empty jars" also to me means sometimes using what you have in your hand you need the help of others, you need the help or the push of others. The widow had the little oil, the seed, something that is the key to her financial crisis but she needed other people's jars to increase the amount of what she had in her hands. Whatever you have and who ever you are in this world you need someone's help, others' assistance to unlock your future, therefore respect what is in other people's hand, trust God and be willing and able to work with others. Even when you are rich enough to establish any kind of business you still need people to work for you.

2 Kings 6:1-7, "And the sons of the prophets said to Elisha, "See now, the place where we dwell with you is too small for us. Please, let us go to the Jordan, and let every man take a beam from there, and let us make there a place where we may dwell." So he answered, "Go." Then one said, "Please consent to go with your servants." And he answered, "I will go." So he went with them. And when they came to the Jordan, they cut down trees. But as one was cutting down a tree, the iron *ax head* fell into the water; and he cried out and said, "Alas, master! For it was borrowed." So the man of God said, "Where did it fall?" And he showed him the place. So he cut off a stick, and threw *it* in there; and he made the iron float. Therefore he said, "Pick *it* up for yourself." So he reached out his hand and took it." (NKJV)

This wonderful story of the prophet Elisha and the sons of the prophets is also another proof that sometimes it takes the help of others or other people's materials in order for one to use what is in his hand or to execute his vision. The sons of the prophets had a wonderful vision to expand their dwelling place but after obtaining permission from their master the prophet they also needed tools to cut wood so one of them had to go and borrow an axe from a neighbour just as the widow did by going for jars but this time the bible says that in the process of cutting the wood, the head of the borrowed axe fell into river Jordan. Verses 6 and 7 record one of the greatest miracles in the bible where the prophet cut off a stick, and threw it into the river where the axe fell; and the iron floated and appeared on the surface.

The above biblical stories are clear indications that you can succeed not only with what you have but also by using what others have, with the help of others. Nobody was born knowing how to read and write that led them to become a medical doctor, scientist, teacher or an engineer. Nobody was born with a degree or certificate in his/her hand; everyone has to go to school to be taught by a teacher from books other people have written, that is, tapping into other people's knowledge. For anybody to become a mechanic, tailor or seamstress or any other trade work or profession, one has to be an apprentice, spend time learning it from someone who knows how. This is why education is so important in life. To acquire knowledge will add value to whatever you have or know. Your future is in your hand, God has given you a gift or talent, he has given you a seed but you need other people's help so go for it.

Many people today unlike the widow and the sons of prophet pays no attention to what God has given them, they don't know that their future is in their own hands, they are sitting on pots of gold which they despise as nothing. Others also have no respect for what others can do to help them. As a result they have plunged into serious hardship. Unlike this woman who knew what the prophet could do and so went to him for help, many people don't seem to see any way out even though many are Christians who could go to God in prayer to seek for help. As I advise you never to despise the little you have I also say in the same way humbly respect and receive the help others can offer you. Don't say I am older, richer or more educated than them because no matter who you are, you don't possess everything. Elisha was the prophet but it was the sons of the prophet who saw the need for expansion. Sometimes you may need advice from someone. Some people hardly take advice not even from their own wives or husbands. These people always find themselves in troubles which they could have averted if they had discussed it with someone.

To end this chapter, I would like to thank God for many men and women of God he has given to us today whose books I read and also listen to their preaching and teaching which helps me a lot. I learn from these people of their style, the quotations they offer as well as the revelation they bring. Also to become an author writing books, I needed someone's advice, to be able to produce my work. I also needed others to direct me and needed an editor to edit my manuscript. I can say I am not the same as I used to be ten years ago because I have acquired knowledge from others; you can also achieve whatever dream you have by seeking to tap into other people's resources.

The Disciples

Until they came to the master, the disciples did not know they had enough food to feed 5,000 men without women and children counted. It's my prayer that the Lord will open your eyes so that you can see how valuable you are and what you can do. All those you see out there came out of mediocrity and began to climb the ladder of success. Lift yourself from the bottom of that ladder of your success and begin to climb and the Lord who gives the increase will assist you with the things and people you need to make it to the top. It is not going to be easy or a day's job but trust me; gradually you will also make it and burst into fame. Just go to him for direction.

Matthew 14:13-21 (NKJV) reads:

"When Jesus heard *it*, He departed from there by boat to a deserted place by Himself. But when the multitudes heard it, they followed Him on foot from the cities. And when Jesus went out He saw a great multitude; and He was moved with compassion for them, and healed their sick. When it was evening, His disciples came to Him, saying, "This is a deserted place, and the hour is already late. Send the multitudes away, that they may go into the villages and buy themselves food." But Jesus said to them, "They do not need to go away. You give them something to eat." And they said to Him, "We have here only five loaves and two fish." He said, "Bring them here to Me." Then He commanded the multitudes to sit down on the grass. And He took the five loaves and the two fish, and looking up to heaven, He blessed and broke and gave the loaves to the disciples; and the disciples gave to the multitudes. So they all ate and were filled, and they took up twelve baskets full of the fragments that remained. Now those who had eaten were about five thousand men, besides women and children."

In the above story the Scripture says that the disciples used the five loaves of bread and two fish (belonging to a young boy as recorded by John in John 6:9 of the same story) after Jesus had blessed it to feed five thousand men besides women and children, which means that women and children were not counted as it was a Jewish culture at the time. The story also says after everybody was filled they took up twelve baskets full of fragments and of the fish. The point I am trying to make from the story is that before this miracle happened from the other gospel accounts of the same story, Jesus asked the disciples 'what do you have?' and the disciples replied "We have here only five loaves and two fish." This means that before you increase or multiply in your gift, talent or seed you must first recognise and begin with the little that you have and God will bless it to be abundant.

✺

The Critical Importance Of Using What You Have

✳

In the previous chapter, we read about biblical characters operating in their gifts or taking advantage of the opportunities to do so. Now, with their experiences in mind, let's personalise it and look at the importance of using what we have as individuals today.

The 'Parable of the Talents' in Matthew 25:14-30 is given to illustrate the way in which our Lord Jesus will judge men on His return; men who failed to follow His instruction when He left the earth to: 'occupy until I come' (Luke 19:13).

Yet, I believe the parable also clearly demonstrates the importance and rewards of our using what we have; and improving on it – to the benefit of the Kingdom of God. It makes clear what happens when we neglect or fail to use our talents and don't take advantage of opportunities presented to us to do good to and for others. Bearing this in mind, it is true that your gifts could also include financial wealth, but the significance of the 'talents' in the parable is not solely in its great monetary value. It's clear that figuratively 'talents' represent whatever gifts God has given us for the benefit of the Body of Christ and His Kingdom and the fact that a 'talent' is equated to a great deal of money, illustrates how valuable our talents are and that our financial wealth is a part of our 'gift package'. As we use or invest our talents in the Kingdom, just like monetary investments, our talents grow and have a reward or return. Those of us in Christ must realise that we are merely stewards of the gifts and talents we are given when we are born again, and those we have naturally.

> "Each one should use whatever gift he has received to serve others, faithfully administering God's grace in its various forms." - 1 Peter 4:10

Matthew 25:14, the very first verse of the parable, says that the merchant:

> "...called his own servants, and delivered to them his goods." KJV

He didn't give them 'talents' for themselves; he gave them *'his goods'* to use for *his benefit*! Likewise, we are given the responsibility to diligently and faithfully use God's 'wealth', His gifts in us, entrusted to us for Him. Luke 12:42-43 says:

> "And the Lord said, "Who then is that faithful and wise steward, whom his master will make ruler over his household, to give them their portion of food in due season? Blessed is that servant whom his master will find so doing when he comes." NKJV

This is diligence. In the third book of this title you can read about 'The Benefits of Diligence' and the fact that using our diverse gifts diligently, is the secret to a materially and spiritually prosperous life.

We must also realise that we are not only stewards of His gifts, we are just like the servants in the parable who had a *'master'*.

Once we have presented ourselves to God and become born again, we are the Lord's bondservants:

> "Do you not know that to whom you present yourselves slaves to obey, you are that one's slaves whom you obey, whether of sin leading to death, or of obedience leading to righteousness? But God be thanked that though you were slaves of sin, yet you obeyed from the heart that form of doctrine to which you were delivered. And having been set free from sin, you became slaves of righteousness." - Romans 6:16-18 NKJV

1 Corinthians 6:19-20 puts it this way:

> "Or do you not know that your body is the temple of the Holy Spirit who is in you, whom you have from God, and you are not your own? For you were bought at a price; therefore glorify God in your body and in your spirit, which are God's." NKJV

Just take a moment to think about this. Are you like the two good and faithful servants who took their 'talents' and 'invested' them (did something with them!), and got a return for and from their master? Or are you like the foolish servant who buried his talent, didn't use it because he didn't want his master to benefit, and he didn't want to take a risk himself? I find it very sad and frustrating when you see someone who is obviously talented or gifted in some way who is not using or living up to that ability, thereby, missing out on spiritual and material prosperity. It is one of the main reasons why I wrote this book in the first place! Remember what Matthew 25:29 warns us:

> "For to everyone who has, more will be given, and he will have abundance; but from him who does not have, even what he has will be taken away." NKJV

I don't want to shout from the rooftops a 'hell fire and brimstone' type message, but the parable does say that each of the servants were called to give an account of his use of the talents entrusted to him. I firmly believe that we too will one day have to give an account of what we have been given and what we used it for.

Romans 14:10-12 puts it like this:

> "You, then, why do you judge your brother? Or why do you look down on your brother? For we will all stand before God's judgment seat. It is written:" 'As surely as I live,' says the Lord, 'every knee will bow before me; every tongue will confess to God.' "So then, each of us will give an account of himself to God."

The parable goes on to tell us about what happened to the 'unprofitable servant' in Matthew 25:30; and it is a stark warning to us all!

> "And cast the unprofitable servant into the outer darkness. There will be weeping and gnashing of teeth." NKJV

The scary part of this is that all we have to do to end up in the 'furnace of fire' is to continue to do absolutely nothing with our gifts – there's no effort involved!

My final point in this chapter is that a seed needs to be sown before it prospers, that is, grows and produces fruit! I'll deal with this subject in more depth in the second book, Part 2 of 'What is in Your Hands?' I said at the beginning of the book, I do not want you to be ignorant concerning gifts (1 Corinthians 12:1b), so read what Galatians 6:7-8, NKJV says:

> "Do not be deceived, God is not mocked; for whatever a man sows, that he will also reap. For he who sows to his flesh will of the flesh reap corruption, but he who sows to the Spirit will of the Spirit reap everlasting life." and James 4:17 also says: "Therefore, to him who knows to do good and does not do it, to him it is sin." NKJV

You have been warned!

Seed

Someone may be waiting to get something big before beginning to do something with it but I want you to know that irrespective of how you see yourself and your excuses, the Lord has not given up on you like you have yet; He says there is something in your hand he has given you. It is a seed that holds the future of your life. Many people could have been happy and successful in life than they are now if they had realized and worked with the little seed that they have for a seed will remain single until it is planted or developed. A lot of people for lack of confidence and value for what is in their hands are doing other things which are less beneficial and less progressive. Even many nations who have been blessed with many natural resources that could have made its citizens happier and dependable due to improper use of these natural resources and to some due to selfishness in the part of few people in power, the majority of the citizens of these nations are poor and some of them who are able to migrate to other countries end up as economic refugees.

Knowing what you have

'How would I know what I hold - my future, my seed, tool, gift or talent in my hand', someone may ask? If this is your question I direct you to go to God in prayer and he will direct you. Knowing that God is the source of all that we need in this life and a father who is ready and willing to give to his children whatever they ask him at anytime and therefore go to him in times of any need such as how to know what is in your hand will help you to realise what you have. For not until you know what you have you cannot operate in it. You can only use what you have when you know you have it. Solomon in his wisdom said God gives wisdom and victory to those who keep the commandments of God:

> "My son, if you accept my words and store
> up my commands within you, turning your
> ear to wisdom and applying your heart to
> understanding, and if you call out for insight and
> cry aloud for understanding, and if you look for it
> as for silver and search for it as for hidden treasure,
> then you will understand the fear of the Lord and
> find the knowledge of God. For the Lord gives

wisdom, and from his mouth come knowledge and understanding. He holds victory in store for the upright, he is a shield to those whose walk is blameless,"
- Proverbs 2:1-7 (ANIV)

Jesus said,

"Ask, and it will be given to you; seek, and you will find; knock, and it will be opened to you." - Matthew 7:7 (NKJV)

James said,

"If any of you lacks wisdom, let him ask of God, who gives to all liberally and without reproach, and it will be given to him." - James 1:5 (NKJV)

Another practical answer or direction I will give you if you are wondering what could be your gift or talent or something the Lord has placed in your hand is, "Is there anything you know in your life that you can do so easily even though others find it difficult to do? Or is there anything you love to do more than doing any other thing because whatever the Lord gives to you to do he gives you also the direction and the means to do. I know I am called as a minister of God to preach and teach his word because even though I went to school and qualified as a motor vehicle technician and have also done many jobs, I find it easy and take pleasure to serve God in preaching and teaching his word than doing other things in life for I have come to know that you will excel in doing what the Lord has called you to do than doing any other work in life.

Knowing and doing your God-given job

I know people who work many hours, seven days a week with less time to rest, not even time with their family and more or less time with God but with nothing to show for their round the clock toil because they have drifted from their God-given work. Drifting from your God given call or job could make you work so hard with long hours but less progress: Some jobs and office could be more attracting but might not be your God-given job. Many times we refuse what God intend for us then go our own way which does not help us. Doing what you have been called to do is the best thing to do. Never allow what is in your hand to be wasted; do something with it. I would like to use the stories below to throw more light on knowing and doing your God-given job or what the Lord has placed in your hands.

Key Quotations: Luke 5:1-11 (4-10); John 21:1-5 (3-6)

Luke 5:1-11 (4-11),

"When he had finished speaking, he said to Simon, "Put out into deep water, and let down the net for a catch" (5) Simon answered, "Master we've worked hard all night and haven't caught anything. But because you say so, I will let down the net." When they had done so, they caught such a large number of fish that their net began to break, so they signalled their partners in the other boat to come and help them, and they came and filled both boats so full that they began to sink. When Simon Peter saw this, he fell at Jesus' knees and said, "Go away from me, Lord; I am sinful man!" For he and all his companions were astonished at the catch of fish they had taken, and so were James and John, the sons of Zebedee, Simon's partners. Then Jesus said to Simon, ***"Don't be afraid; from now on you will catch men."***

John 21 (3-6),

3. "I'm going out to fish," Simon Peter told them, and they said, "We'll go with you." So they went out and got into the boat, but that night they caught nothing.
4. Early in the morning, Jesus stood on the shore, but the disciples did not realize that it was Jesus,
5. He called out to them, "Friends, haven't you any fish?" "No," they answered.
6. He said, "Throw your net on the right side of the boat and you will find some." When they did, they were unable to haul the net in because of the large number of fish.

Vss. 7-14 when they realised it was Jesus, he had breakfast with them

Vss. 15-18 Jesus challenges Peter with this question "Do you love me?"

Backgrounds of Both key quotations Luke 5:1-11 (4-10); John 21:1-5 (3-6)

First in Luke

Peter and his colleagues with all their experience in fishing caught nothing having worked all night (doing things on their own way). Jesus comes in, tells them to do it his way; even though it was not the right hour for fishing in the eyes of men but that yielded fruit. Having caught their attention Jesus commissioned Peter with a new responsibility **"from now on you will catch men."** That is you'll no more be working on fish but you will be fishing for men to bring them into the kingdom of God.

Secondly in John

Again Peter and other disciples after Jesus' death decided to go their own way to fishing and again it was fruitless, they caught nothing. Then again Jesus came in and directed them to where they belong and again they got so much fish that their own way could not get. Jesus then challenged Peter three times, "Do you love me" which Peter responded in each case "yes Lord" "you know that I love you" Jesus again said "feed my lamb, feed my sheep, and feed my lamb, that is, you say you love me; prove your love through your service which is doing what I have commanded you (to catch men).

Even though this is purely spiritual I would like to bring it into the natural. Like Peter if Jesus appears to you and ask you now "Do you love me?" what will be your answer? I know for sure many will say like Peter "I love you Lord" but your actions will differ from what you say. Most times when we hear things like Peter's story we make all sorts of statements e.g. how could Peter not do what the Lord commanded him? My answer is; are you doing what he wants you to do? In the same way in most cases when we hear the word of God been preached, we turn to refer it to others and say it would have been very good if 'Mr so and so' were here; we refuse to receive it for ourselves. This reminds me of Paul's statement to the Romans. He said,

> "You, therefore, have no excuse, you who pass judgment on someone else, for at whatever point you judge the other, you are condemning yourself, because you who pass judgment do the same things. - Romans 2:1 (ANIV)

Without any doubt God has given to everyone a specific work in both the spiritual and physical (John 15:16). But the question is: are you doing what you have been given or called to do or you have drifted and going your own way? This is the reason so many of us having tried so hard so long still we are not getting anywhere. How do you think? Are you on the right track both in your spiritual life and physical life? **In Spiritual life I mean:** Your walk with God, your Christian life. Are you doing what you have been called to do? Which gift are you operating on in the body of Christ? **In Physical I mean:** Your physical life, do you also think you are on your right job. Doing the right job becomes so easy and enjoying. No matter how long you work you can make a meaningful life out of it. Like I said before some jobs and offices could be could be more attracting but might not be your God-given job. Sadly enough, many are confused not knowing what to do both spiritually and physically.

- Some don't have any clue about what is expected of them
- Others also know but think doing other things will help them so they are going their own way

To end this part of this book my advice to the first group is to seek God to know what you have been called to do and to the second go back to what you know is your call or what is in your hand. Don't go your own way; it will be waste of time and energy. Peter and his friends worked all night but caught nothing until they came back to the original recommended by the master. I have come to know as I said earlier on that I am called to preach so all my life is all about preaching. I am always looking for statements and matters to preach with. I dream about it, I talk about it and enjoy doing it. What about you? Look and stick to what you've been called to do; it may seem little or insignificant but what you don't know is it is just a seed and seed never grow until it is planted.

Jesus asked Peter "do you love me?" take care of my sheep. If Jesus pays you a visit now, would you be commended or you will be condemned for what you are doing both in your spiritual and physical life? If your answer is not right change before is too late.

I have seen many people in the kingdom of God even ministers who could have been doing great for the Lord through the gift God have given them but are now doing different things with no Holy Spirit backing because they are going their own way not the Lord's way. I have also seen those who are trying to be everything and as a result cannot excel in any of them. I would like to take this opportunity to advice my fellow ministers who are called to be pastors and teachers which may not be attractive and respectful in the eyes of many these days like other gifts not to follow money and recognition from men to digress from what the Lord has called them to be for he who has called you will also reward you irrespective of how unpopular your gift may be no matter what the temptation is.

Also know that preachers and teachers are very important in the kingdom of God because without them, people will not hear the word and come to salvation as Paul wrote to the Roman Church. He said,

> "How then shall they call on Him in whom they have not believed? And how shall they believe in Him of whom they have not heard? And how shall they hear without a preacher?" - Romans 10:14 (NKJV)

Quoting Deuteronomy 25:4 from the Old Testament, Paul again said preachers and teachers must be well paid showing that preachers and teachers are very important in the body of Christ even though some of the other ministerial gifts are more popular and are well cared for in these days.

> "The elders who direct the affairs of the church well are worthy of double honour, especially those whose work is preaching and teaching. For the Scripture says, "Do not muzzle the ox while it is treading out the grain," and "The worker deserves his wages." - 1 Timothy 5:17-18 (ANIV)

Be proud of yourself and be joyful in your work and in your calling for you are special in the sight of God.

As I said earlier on, many would have excelled if they had stuck to what the Lord had given them but they followed the crowd, they followed their mind not their heart. I know the temptation to change what you are doing especially when things are not going well but I also know that God will always prosper what he has given. Therefore I advice you to stick to what you have (your gift or talent) and God will bless you.

Protecting your seed

As unprotected valuable belongings can be destroyed or stolen so also are our gifts and talents so you must look properly after what the Lord has given you and protect it, for the enemy has destroyed many people's seed, that is, what they have in their hand, because they were unprotected. Whatever you see as your seed needs to be protected and cared for. The Scripture says

> "The thief does not come except to steal, and to kill, and to destroy. I have come that they may have life, and that they may have *it* more abundantly." (John 10:10)

Ask God in prayer all the time to protect your seed from the enemy. Other ways of protecting what you have is to acknowledge that God is the source, the centre and the end of all that you have and give him the glory for any success. Failure to do so and taking the glory to yourself, you risk yourself making what you have vulnerable to the enemy to destroy. So many people have lost gifts and talents because they left God behind. Another way to protect your seed or what is in your hand is to plant it, which is to use it. So, do your part by planting your seed and God will also do his part by bringing the increase as Paul said,

"I planted, Apollos watered, but God gave the increase." (1 Corinthians 3:6)

When you plant your seed he will water it.

"For as the rain comes down, and the snow from heaven, And do not return there, But water the earth, And make it bring forth and bud, That it may give seed to the sower And bread to the eater, So shall My word be that goes forth from My mouth; It shall not return to Me void, But it shall accomplish what I please, And it shall prosper *in the thing* for which I sent it." (Isaiah 55:10-11)

With my background born and brought up in a farming community, I have seen many times when people have suffered great loss because their crops were destroyed by some animals and some birds. Crops like corn, cassava, rice are most likely to be destroyed by these animals unless the farm is protected by traps around the farm. Some farms need a constant noise to deter birds from destroying the crops. Interesting enough the farmer who is able to put up traps around his farm not only protects his crops but also benefits from catching these animals and eat them as meat. Don't leave your seed free for the enemy; put up trap of prayers around it. Another way of protecting what the Lord has given you is to be able to control your tongue by not revealing all details about what you have because it's not everybody who will be happy when you prosper. Those who will wish your downfall may find ways to destroy your seed as some animals and some birds will destroy some crops so be vigilant and wise as to whom you must disclose or expose details of your gift or talent. I have seen many who received bad counselling and directives from those who they think were helping them even people who were very close to them.

Also to protect your seed, what is in your hand, your gift or talent is to look after your body and life style very well. What you eat or drink and even what you say must be on your priority list because what you eat, drink or say can ruin your life or destroy your gift or talent. I have seen many gifted and talented people whose careers have been destroyed because they failed to look after their body well. I know many musicians and footballers who were heroes and idols for many but ended up in shame and in poverty as a result of bad habits such as alcoholism and gambling; they failed to protect what they have and so the devil destroyed it. As you read this book I want you to take notes and learn lessons before you say 'had I known' for it is said "Had I known is always at last." Acknowledge anything in your life you see as a blessing from the Lord and use it diligently and your future will be bright.

Samson had his world at his finger tips, a man born a Nazarite unto God, a man born with the ability to deliver his people Israel from the hands of their enemies the Philistines but he lost all because the Spirit of God (his physical strength) left him which resulted in him being captured by the enemies who gauged out his two eyes because he failed to protect what the Lord had given him with his encounter with Delilah who betrayed him. Judges 16:20-21 says:

> "Then she called, "Samson, the Philistines are upon you!" He awoke from his sleep and thought, "I'll go out as before and shake myself free." But he did not know that the Lord had left him. Then

the Philistines seized him, gouged out his eyes and took him down to Gaza. Binding him with bronze shackles, they set him to grinding in the prison."
(ANIV)

Finally he perished in the last destruction he brought upon his enemies as recorded in Judges 16:28-30:

"Then Samson prayed to the LORD, "O Sovereign LORD, remember me. O God, please strengthen me just once more, and let me with one blow get revenge on the Philistines for my two eyes." Then Samson reached towards the two central pillars on which the temple stood. Bracing himself against them, his right hand on the one and his left hand on the other, Samson said, "Let me die with the Philistines!" Then he pushed with all his might, and down came the temple on the rulers and all the people in it. Thus he killed many more when he died than while he lived." (ANIV)

For more details about the story of Samson read Judges Chapter 13-16. One of the saddest parts of his story is the fact that for 20 years as a judge that he led Israel, the

Scripture records more of his mistakes and failures than his accomplishments. Samson had a great potential many people may not have but wasted it and he suffered as a result when he lost his physical strength the Lord gave him. I hope with a lesson from Samson's life you'll be wise enough to look after what is in your hand properly and be mindful of the people you associate yourself with. I advice that you look for people who will help you to protect your future not those who will contribute to the destruction of what is in your hand. Also remember Samson was born to strengthen his people and show them the way to the Lord. He could have destroyed the enemy to set his people free but he wasted all these abilities because of a woman who pretended to love him. Like Samson you have also been born into your family or nation not by chance or by accident but for a divine purpose. Perhaps, through what the Lord has given you, you will lead your people to God, bring financial freedom to your family. Think about this! I have seen and heard of many people who came from very obscure backgrounds but sprung up to fame and became well to do because they discovered their gifts and talent.

✹

Some Of The Reasons Why People Fail To Recognise Or Use What They Have

Until you know who you are or what you have in your hand, all you possess, your armour and strength becomes valueless. Fear and despising what you have can cause you to build up events, even pictures in your mind that will cause you to disqualify yourself or cause you to be defeated even before you attempt to do anything in life. Before you can move on in life or use what you have in your hand in this context you must be able to overcome all negative thoughts some of which I am going to discuss.

1. Discouragements from others:

Discouragement as we know is an act of somebody that tends to prevent something from happening by making it more difficult or unpleasant to try to stop a person or animal from doing something; to make somebody feel less motivated, confident, or optimistic. For this reason advising parents in his instructions to Christian households how to live Paul said,

> "Fathers, do not embitter your children, or they will become discouraged." Colossians 3:21 (ANIV)

NLT puts it this way,

> "Father's don't aggravate your children. If you do, they will become discouraged and quit trying."

Paul is saying to parents that by discouraging your children, you cause them to stop or quit trying to do what they want to do. Children have a more positive approach and the willingness to try again when they are encouraged. Therefore it is the responsibility of every parent who expects that their children do well in life to encourage not to discourage them even when they are at fault or mistaken.

Are your actions or what you say to others or your children encouraging or discouraging?

Many have quit trying to use their gifts and talents because they were discouraged by others. To some because of what was said to them have made them bitter another obstacle to people using what God has given them. I have heard many times in church of this scenario when people have refused to try again to use their gifts and talents because of how others reacted to them when they tried to operate in their gifts. Some of these individuals were laughed at which got them offended. Offence is one of the powerful tools the enemy uses to deny people from reaching their potential because an angry person not only refuses to use his gift or talent but in most cases also becomes an opposition and therefore stops people also from doing what he has refused to do which I believe is an act that brings the wrath of God.

Examples of discouragement and how some people overcame them

Hannah overcame her discouragement with prayer: The Full story is from verse 1. 1 Samuel 1:10-11 (ANIV),

"In bitterness of soul Hannah wept much and prayed to the Lord. "And she made a vow, saying, "O Lord Almighty, if you will only look upon your servant's misery and remember me, and not forget your servant but give her a son, then I will give him to the Lord for all the days of his life, and no razor will ever be used on his head."

1 Samuel 1:6-7 (NKJV),

"And her rival also provoked her severely, to make her miserable, because the Lord had closed her womb. So it was, year by year, when she went up to the house of the Lord, that she provoked her; therefore she wept and did not eat."

1 Samuel 1:13-17 (ANIV),

"Hannah was praying in her heart, and her lips were moving but her voice was not heard. Eli thought she was drunk and said to her, "How long will you keep on getting drunk?

Get rid of your wine." "Not so, my lord," Hannah replied, "I am a woman who is deeply troubled. I have not been drinking wine or beer; I was pouring out my soul to the LORD. Do not take your servant for a wicked woman; I have been praying here out of my great anguish and grief." Eli answered, "Go in peace, and may the God of Israel grant you what you have asked of him."

What could be more discouraging to a woman being the first wife but with no children when her husband's second wife always provokes and makes her miserable because she had more children to boast of. The worse of all was when Hannah went to the house of God to pray and the man of God accused her of been drunk with wine but with her humble response, she went home with a promise to have her heart's desire within a year. And it came to pass as the man of God had told her

---

"Go in peace, and may the God of Israel grant you what you have asked of him."

People may have ridiculed you the first time, even several occasions that you made an attempt to do something with what you believe to be your gift or talent so you have coiled back; get back and try again. Never allow discouragement from others to deter you for you will be burying your fortune.

King David:

King David did not allow situation to weigh him down but strengthened himself in the Lord. In the context of this book he was not discouraged with the situation around him but encouraged himself in the Lord.

Key Quotation:

1 Samuel 30:1-6, "Now it happened, when David and his men came to Ziklag, on the third day, that the Amalekites had invaded the South and Ziklag, attacked Ziklag and burned it with fire, and had taken captive the women and those who *were* there, from small to great; they did not kill anyone, but carried *them* away and went their way. So David and his men came to the city, and there it was, burned with fire; and their wives, their sons, and their daughters had been taken captive. Then

David and the people who *were* with him lifted up their voices and wept, until they had no more power to weep. And David's two wives, Ahinoam the Jezreelitess, and Abigail the widow of Nabal the Carmelite, had been taken captive. Now David was greatly distressed, for the people spoke of stoning him, because the soul of all the people was grieved, every man for his sons and his daughters. But David strengthened himself in the LORD his God."

Background:

King David and his men went to war and on their return they found that the enemy, the Amalekites had invaded their city Ziklag, bent it and their children and wives taken away including David's two wives. Verse 6 says out of desperation the people turned against David and even planned to kill him even though he had also lost two wives. This is a typical example of how difficult it is to be a leader; when things goes right we all share the glory but when it goes wrong everyone turns against the leader.

But in the midst of the revolt from his people, the loss of his two wives, the Amplified Bible says in verse 6 last sentence,

> "But David encouraged and strengthened himself in the Lord",

in other words David sort strength from the Lord his God. He did not allow the situation to weigh him down but he turned to the Lord knowing that God is the only one who could help him at that time. As he encouraged and strengthened himself in the Lord he had the strength to pray to God for direction (Vs 8). Then in Vss. 18-19, he recovered everything the enemy (the Amalekites) took from them as he followed the direction the Lord showed him.

Notice something very important and useful:

Regardless of his loss (his people including his two wives), David did not seek counsel from men but encouraged or strengthened himself in the Lord, then sought direction from the Lord. The result was he recovered everything. In relating this story of David and his men to our personal present life, I would like to ask you: What is your position now? What problem do you find yourself in? How are you handling it? Are you capitulated by it or you are in control? What has the enemy stolen from you? Who has turned against you and why? What seems to discourage you?

For David the enemy invaded, bent his city and took away some women and children including his two wives when he and his people were out to war. One of the greatest discouragements in life but when he refused to be discouraged and turned to the Lord he found strength to recover all that he lost. I also want to encourage you as you read this book that if you want to move on in life, I believe one of the key factors is to encourage yourself in the Lord irrespective of the situation you find yourself in for I also believe if you fail to encourage yourself no one can do it for you. Another way to encourage yourself in the Lord is to make yourself happy but unfortunately some people look to others for happiness. Another thing you may not know is that the one you may be looking to for your happiness may even be the one behind your trouble. Don't give in to your problems but look to God for solutions like David.

2. Fear:

King Saul and Israel's Army: Through fear of Goliath, the people of Israel including King

Saul forgot that they had a covenant with God which means that they are fully protected by God until a shepherd boy, David who knew who he is came in to defeat Goliath with a single stone out of the five stones he had (1 Samuel 17). David knew as an Israelite, he had a covenant with God with his circumcision that made him special over the uncircumcised Philistine giant. The Israelites including their King were totally paralyzed for forty days because of the powerful words of Goliath. In the same way many people because of fear have refused to make a move in life or use what they have as gifts or talents or any material thing they have. Many believe when they do, they will fail, lose or flop because of the nature of the challenge they face.

Even though there may be so much against you, I encourage you it's not how you see yourself but how God sees you. You are a man or a woman of valour, worth more than you see yourself. Renew your mind with a positive mindset. May God open your mind to know as he did to the servant of Elisha for you to know that greater is he that is in you than he that is in the world and you will no longer be afraid of the multitude of enemies that come against you.

> "When the servant of the man of God got up and went out early the next morning, an army with horses and chariots had surrounded the city."Oh, my lord, what shall we do?" the servant asked. "Don't be afraid," the prophet answered. "Those who are with us are more than those who are with them." And Elisha prayed, "O LORD, open his eyes so that he may see." Then the LORD opened the servant's eyes, and he looked and saw the hills full of horses and chariots of fire all round Elisha." - 2 Kings 6:15-17 (ANIV)

The apostle John said,

> "You are of God, little children, and have overcome them, because He who is in you is greater than he who is in the world." - 1 John 4:4 (NKJV)

3. Inferiority complex:

This is when a person has the sense of being inferior to other people. In extreme cases it can manifest itself in either withdrawn or aggressive social behaviour. I believe when a person is affected with inferiority complex he becomes fearful of something or someone and they begin to feel inferior before the thing or the one like the story below: Out of fear ten out of the twelve spies came out with a bad report.

"And they returned from spying out the land after forty days. Now they departed and came back to Moses and Aaron and all the congregation of the children of Israel in the Wilderness of Paran, at Kadesh; they brought back word to them and to all the congregation, and showed them the fruit of the land. Then they told him, and said: "We went to the land where you sent us. It truly flows with milk and honey, and this *is* its fruit. Nevertheless the people who dwell in the land *are* strong; the cities *are* fortified *and* very large; moreover we saw the descendants of Anak there. The Amalekites dwell in the land of the South; the Hittites, the Jebusites, and the Amorites dwell in the mountains; and the Canaanites dwell by the sea and along the banks of the Jordan." Then Caleb quieted the people before Moses, and said, "Let us go up at once and take possession, for we are well able to overcome it." But the men who had gone up with him said, "We are not able to go up against the people, for they *are* stronger than we." And they gave the children of Israel a bad report of the land which they had spied out, saying, "The land through which we have gone as spies *is* a land that devours its inhabitants, and all the people whom we saw in it *are* men of *great* stature. There we saw the giants (the descendants of Anak

came from the giants); and we were like grasshoppers in our own sight, and so we were in their sight."
(Numbers 13:25-33)

The ten spies out of inferiority complex that developed into fear forgot all the Lord had done for them for all those years in the wilderness, and also overlooked all the goodness they saw in the land and their negative perception told them they are nothing but like grasshoppers in our own sight and so we were in their sight. Notice something they said: 'we were like grasshoppers not only in our sight but also in the sight of the inhabitants too;' what a shame. My advice to you is: may the Lord grant you the spirit of Joshua and Caleb that made the difference.

"Then Caleb quieted the people before Moses, and said, "Let us go up at once and take possession, for we are well able to overcome it."

You see the Lord had given them the land, it was already in their hand and they were only to go and posses but lack of confidence in God and in themselves due to what they saw prevented them. If you want to be able to use what you have, you must do away with mediocrity mindset and begin to believe in God and in yourself and you will be who God wants you to be.

4. Lack of confidence:

(Lack of self assurance or a belief in your ability to succeed) Lack of confidence will always make you struggle with new challenges and in fact people make excuses and try to avoid taking on new challenges or use what God has given them because of lack of confidence, because they don't believe in themselves. Many will say "I am not well-educated enough, I am poor, because of my colour; I am not worthy or good enough. You need to believe in yourself that you are also somebody, a child of God who by right, that is, through Jesus Christ you are able to succeed at everything you try to do for with him all things are possible. Do you remember from our foundation Scripture that despite God's instruction to 'Come now therefore, and I will send thee'; and His constant step-by-step instructions and reassurances to Moses he persists in questioning God, raising objections and making excuses is all due to the fact that he did not have confidence in himself. He did not believe he could do anything especially such a great task the Lord was giving. Also remember that whenever God gives you a task he will also give you provision or the help to carry that task. So never feel lonely or intimidated trying to use your gift for the Lord is with you.

Jeremiah said,

> "Ah, Sovereign LORD," I said, "I do not know how to speak; I am only a child." But the LORD said to me, "Do not say, 'I am only a child.' You must go to everyone I send you to and say whatever I command you. Do not be afraid of them, for I am with you and will rescue you," declares the LORD." - Jeremiah 1:6-8 (ANIV)

Often people struggle with new challenges because they lack self-confidence, feeling that they have inadequate ability, training, or experience. From the above story, Jeremiah thought he was "too young" and inexperienced to be God's prophet to the nations. But God promised to be with him. We should not allow feelings of inadequacy to keep us from obeying God and be ready to take up a challenge. God will always be with us. If God gives you a job to do, he will provide all you need to do it. Taking up a challenge involves hard work and determination; it involves the ability to tolerate others and never give up spirit. Have confidence in yourself and you will make it by the help of God. **Lack of confidence** can develop into inferiority complex, an overdeveloped sense of being inferior to other people. In extreme cases it can manifest itself in either withdrawn or aggressive social behaviour.

Saul:

Lack of confidence caused him to hide even though he was chosen by God to be the first king of Israel, can you believe it?

Key Quotation:

1 Samuel 10:17-24 (NKJV), "Then Samuel called the people together to the LORD at Mizpah, and said to the children of Israel, "Thus says the LORD God of Israel: 'I brought up Israel out of Egypt, and delivered you from the hand of the Egyptians and from the hand of all kingdoms and from those who oppressed you.' "But you have today rejected your God, who Himself saved you from all your adversities and your tribulations; and you have said to Him, 'No, set a king over us!' Now therefore, present yourselves before the LORD by your tribes and by your clans." And when Samuel had caused all the tribes of Israel to come near, the tribe of Benjamin was chosen. When he had caused the tribe of Benjamin to come near by their families, the family of Matri was chosen. And Saul the son of Kish was chosen. But when they sought him, he could not be found. Therefore they inquired of the LORD further, "Has the man come here yet?" And the LORD answered, "There he is, hidden among the equipment." So they ran and brought him from there; and when he stood among the people, he was taller than any of the people from his shoulders upward. And Samuel said to all the people, "Do you see him whom the LORD has chosen, that there is no one like him among all the people?" So all the people shouted and said, "Long live the king!"

Background:

Israel requested for a king: 1 Samuel 8:4-5 (ANIV)

"So all the elders of Israel gathered together and came to Samuel at Ramah. They said to him, "You are old, and your sons do not walk in your ways; now appoint a king to lead us, such as all the other nations have."

Description of Saul:

"There was a man of Benjamin whose name was Kish the son of Abiel, the son of Zeror, the son of Bechorath, the son of Aphiah, a Benjamite, a mighty man of power. And he had a choice and handsome son whose name was Saul. There was not a more handsome person than he among the children of Israel. From his shoulders upward he was taller than any of the people."
- 1 Samuel 9:1-2 (NKJV)

How Saul met Samuel and chose to become the King of Israel: Saul went to look for his father's donkey but found Samuel:

"They went up to the town, and as they were entering it, there was Samuel, coming towards them on his way up to the high place. Now the day before Saul came, the LORD had revealed this to Samuel: "About this time tomorrow I will send you a man from the land of Benjamin. Anoint him leader over my people Israel; he will deliver my people from the hand of the Philistines. I have looked upon my people, for their cry has reached me." When Samuel caught sight of Saul, the LORD said to him, "This is the man I spoke to you about; he will govern my people." 1 Samuel 9:14-17 (ANIV)

Anointed: Then Samuel took a flask of oil and poured it on Saul's head and kissed him, saying,

"Has not the LORD anointed you leader over his inheritance?"

- 1 Samuel 10:1 (ANIV) **But from verse in 21-22,** due to lack of confidence when the Israelites assembled to choose a king, Saul already knew he was the one but instead of coming forward, the Scripture says he hid himself among the baggage even though he was chosen by God. In the context of the theme of this book he refused to 'Move On' with what was already in his hand, his future as a King hiding among baggage.

"When he had caused the tribe of Benjamin to come near by their families, the family of Matri was chosen. And Saul the son of Kish was chosen. But when they sought him, he could not be found. Therefore they inquired of the LORD further, "Has the man come here yet?" And the LORD answered, "There he is, hidden among the equipment."

This reminds me of what Jesus said in his sermon on the Mount. He said,

> "You are the salt of the earth. But if the salt loses its saltiness, how can it be made salty again? It is no longer good for anything, except to be thrown out and trampled by men."

- Matthew 5:13 (ANIV) This means that failure to recognize who you are and use what you have renders you useless and instead of you being given respect and honour you will be despised by men. Imagine what came into the minds of those who found Saul among the baggage. Never miss the opportunity to use what is in your hand; it is the key to your future. Often we hide from important responsibilities or positions, we also refuse to use what is in our hands because we are afraid of failure, afraid of what others will think or say, or perhaps unsure about how to proceed. Prepare now to step up to your future responsibilities. Count on God's provision rather than your feelings of adequacy. I know many who run from responsibilities of using what God has given them as gifts to serve him and as a result the lives of these individuals have not been fulfilling.

In my concluding words I will say if you lose your confidence you cannot move on therefore have confidence in yourself that you can also make it just as others have made it. Stop crying and stop considering yourself inferior, it's time to move on.

- When Moses overcame his lack of confidence, God used him mightily and he is on record as one of the greatest leaders the world had ever seen.
- Jeremiah was not successful in the eyes of people, he was rejected by his own people, put into prison, called 'the weeping prophet, but in the eyes of God Jeremiah was one of the successful people in all of history because he also overcame his lack of confidence.
- Gideon also overcame his lack of confidence and God used him to deliver his people.

Finally, I would also like to say that another reason why some people fail to use what they have in their hand is that they are happy to help others to develop what they have but fail to develop what is their own. These are those who are happy to receive wages from others or been paid by others but would not try to do something themselves that will make them also bosses who can also employ others to work for them. Nevertheless if you think you have nothing in your hand I urge you go to God in prayer and he will reveal to you what he has given to you. Even though it may not be easy trying something on your own as there may be so many obstacles or hindrances on the way but always remember the words of Paul

"being confident of this, that he who began a good work in you will carry it on to completion until the day of Christ Jesus." Philippians 1:6 (ANIV)

The Lord who has given you the gift, talent or seed will see to the success of whatever you try to do with what he has given you

6. Laziness:

In the process of writing this book, one day I felt the Holy Spirit ministering to me as he did to me saying 'Do you know that laziness is also part of the reasons why people fail to recognise what is in their hand and so fail to use them?' Laziness is an act of one not wanting to work, unwilling to work or when one fails to make an effort do something. We live in the world today where people are lazy but want to enjoy life. As a result of laziness false prophets and teachers are taking advantage of and deceiving many who failed to heed to the advise of big brother Paul when he said,

> "I urge you, to watch out for those who cause divisions and put obstacles in your way that are contrary to the teaching you have learned. Keep away from them. For such people are not serving our Lord Jesus Christ, but their own appetites. By smooth talk and flattery they deceive the minds of naïve people." - Romans 16:17-18

As I always say your gift, talent or seed or anything you think you have will be wasted if you are lazy; for laziness will deny anyone of any effort to do something with what they have irrespective of the size or how interesting it may be. King Solomon in Proverbs made it clear that diligence, which is being willing to work hard (opposite of laziness) is very important in human life. Even though when we work hard we do so to become rich, famous or admired by others but what we don't know is most importantly when we work hard we serve God with the gifts and talents he has given us that brings glory to him and that brings his blessings to us. **He said,**

"A hard worker will become" Rich but the lazy will be soon be poor. He said Lazy hands make a man poor, but diligent hands bring wealth. He who gathers crops in summer is a wise son, but he who sleeps during harvest is a disgraceful son. - Proverbs 10:4-5 (ANIV).

Never desire to be rich and don't crave for money if you are lazy but to the diligent I say expect to be rich one day as you continue working hard, but the lazy will be slaves.

"Diligent hands will rule, but laziness ends in slave labour." - Proverbs 12:24 (ANIV).

Those who always try to use what they have will always take advantage of those who fail to do so. Those who fail to use what is in their hand always rely or depend on others that enable them to take advantage over them. Don't allow your laziness to turn you into a slave to someone you are not supposed to. People are cheated in various ways here and there because of the failure to have confidence in using what they have.

Will serve before kings:

"Do you see a man skilled in his work? He will serve before kings; he will not serve before obscure men."

- Proverbs 22:29 (ANIV) Faithfully using what is in your hands will elevate you; it will take you where you never dream of going.

Paul advises the church against laziness:

"But concerning brotherly love you have no need that I should write to you, for you yourselves are taught by God to love one another; and indeed you do so toward all the brethren who are in all Macedonia. But we urge you, brethren, that you increase more and more; that you also aspire to lead a quiet life, to mind your own business, and to work with your own hands, as we commanded you, that you may walk properly toward those who are outside, and *that* you may lack nothing." - 1 Thessalonians 4:9-12 (NKJV)

Other Results of diligence:

Even though it is stressful and discomforting, those who are not lazy but diligent in their work will always reap the abundance or the fruit of their labour.

"He who works his land will have abundant food, but the one who chases fantasies will have his fill of poverty." - Proverbs 28:19 (ANIV)

Paul also said,

"What soldier has to pay his own expenses? And have you ever heard of a farmer who harvests his crop and doesn't have the right to eat some of it? What shepherd takes care of a flock of sheep and isn't allowed to drink some of the milk? And this isn't merely human opinion. Doesn't God's law say the same thing? For the law of Moses says, "Do not keep an ox from eating as it treads out the grain." Do you suppose God was thinking only about oxen when he said this? Wasn't he also speaking to us? Of course he was. Just as farm workers who plow fields and thresh the grain expect a share of the harvest, Christian workers should be paid by those they serve." - 1 Corinthians 9:7-10 (NLT) Paul was referring to Deuteronomy 25:4.

He also advises Timothy and all believers:

"You then, my son, be strong in the grace that is in Christ Jesus. And the things you have heard me say in the presence of many witnesses entrust to reliable men who will also be qualified to teach others. Endure hardship with us like a good soldier of Christ Jesus. No-one serving as a soldier gets involved in civilian affairs—he wants to please his commanding officer. Similarly, if anyone competes as an athlete, he does not receive the victor's crown unless he competes according to the rules. The hardworking farmer should be the first to receive a share of the crops." - 2 Timothy 2:1-6 (ANIV)

You cannot peep through a hole with your two eyes; you can only do when you close one eye.

This means that if you want to be a medical doctor or any highly rated professional you have to cut down your playing and sleeping times in order to have more time for your studies, for you lose one to gain the other. The interesting side is that when you work hard as a farmer you will be the first person to enjoy the fruit of your labour. A child who listen to his or her parents to work hard to achieve good result or better grades in school when offered a good job enjoys his/her wages Paul said.

Peter when he was also advising men and young men said,

> "And the God of all grace, who called you to his eternal glory in Christ, after you have suffered a little while, will himself restore you and make you strong, firm and steadfast." - 1 Peter 5:10 (ANIV)

In the beginning it could be very hard as I said before but there will be joy in the day of harvest. Whatever is in your hand, whatever is your gift, talent or seed you need zeal to grow it. The Psalmist said,

"Those who sow in tears will reap with songs of joy. He who goes out weeping, carrying seed to sow, will return with songs of joy, carrying sheaves with him." - Psalms 126:5-6 (ANIV)

At this time as I prepare to end this part of my message can I ask you again? "What is in your hand?" Is it a trade work, skilful work, academic or educational? What type of gift do you have in your life? Whatever is your answer do it with diligence for laziness will not help you, it is a wrong choice for you. At the time of writing this book school results were out and on the TV news and in the newspapers, the students who were diligent and studied very hard were happy as they had good grades but the lazy ones who had bad results and could not make it to university were not happy. One of the diligent students who was asked in an interview if she was expecting such results replied, "Yes, because I revised very hard, at least the nervous time is over and I can now celebrate with my friends and family." If you are also studying, do so with diligence and you'll also smile one day when the nervous time is over. Can I categorically advise the young ones that you have the opportunity to be all that you want to be in the future. But notice that it takes hard work to get good grades, so, don't be lazy, study and work hard and get good grades and after you receive your results the nervous time will be over and you will be able to celebrate with your family and friends and gain entrance into the university or a good job.

The bottom line is laziness; apart from the fact that you have failed to honour God with your gift or talent, you have also ruined your own life and will only make yourself poor and a slave to others helping them to use what they have and people will always take advantage of you because you rely on them, but the diligent will be rich, leaders and will serve before Kings. Don't waste your gift or talent, do something with it and you will reap the fruit of your labour. Whatever you are doing, do it with diligence and you'll succeed for the lazy will always fail. With laziness you can lose your job and whatever you think you have and even your marriage can be affected no matter how beautiful you are as a woman and vice versa. Notice also that you will never excel in your gift or talent with laziness. Solomon said

"Whatever your hand finds to do, do it with all your might, for in the grave, where you are going, there is neither working nor planning nor knowledge nor wisdom." - Ecclesiastes 9:10 (ANIV)

- What do you think you have in your hand?
- What do you think you are good at?
- What gift or talent do you have?
- Are you a pastor or any leader in the kingdom of God?
- Have you been blessed with brain to study?
- Are you good in business ideas?

You may not have been blessed with brains to study but as a tradesman or woman or with business ideas, whatever it is, take advantage of it, add value to it, use it to the max; it's your future.

Put an effort to work very hard in any position you have in your work, create something for yourself, don't sit idle and say I have nothing to do. I remember creating my own work pattern in my previous work and when I had to leave I was asked by the manager if I could write it down for them so that it could be a pattern for the position for anyone who comes. Work very hard as a man to be able to look after your family, and always remember that your gift, talent or anything you have is a seed which needs to grow. Also note that with laziness you will never excel in anything you do. No matter how talented you are in playing football, athletics or in anything you are gifted in, it will only take diligence to excel.

✷

Be The Person God Wants You To Be:

✳

There are others who fail to use what is in their hand because they live under the shadow of the opinion of others so they fail to be who God wants them to be. These are those who will not do anything in life until they have received advice or approval from others. What most of these people don't know is that not everyone would like them to prosper so most of the advice they offer them could be against their progress. To these people who live by the words of others I say, if you are one of them, as Paul said to Timothy,

> "Let no one despise your youth, but be an example to the believers in word, in conduct, in love, in spirit, in faith, in purity. Till I come, give attention to reading, to exhortation, to doctrine. Do not neglect the gift that is in you, which was given to you by prophecy with the laying on of the hands of the eldership. Meditate on these things; give yourself entirely

to them, that your progress may be evident to all. Take heed to yourself and to the doctrine. Continue in them, for in doing this you will save both yourself and those who hear you."
(1 Timothy 4:12-16)

Never despise who you are or what you can do. Some of these people you may look to advice you in any step you take may fill your heart with discouragement, fear and doubt. Until we are able to help ourselves we cannot help others, until you become convinced of what you have and what you can do, you will remain a waste until Jesus comes. Before you can be able to use your gift or talent you must first realize or recognise it and also acknowledge that it's been given to you by God. So many have failed to realize what they have and so fighting for what is for others. Seed will forever be single until it is sown. Someone is waiting to get big seed before using it but notice that every big thing began with a small dream. Jesus said,

---

"Most assuredly, I say to you, unless a grain of wheat falls into the ground and dies, it remains alone; but if it dies, it produces much grain." (John 12:24)

Others also fail to use what they have because they compare themselves to others and want to do what someone or others are doing as the Israelites did in the days of Samuel when they rejected him as their leader and demanded him to give them a king as the nations around them. Years ago when I used to be a youth leader in one of our prayers for Holy Spirit baptism, one of my youth members was baptised and spoke in tongues. Some days later he came to me and said he has stopped speaking in tongues because comparing the tongues he speaks to what others speak he found his one inferior so he has stopped. I had to spend some time educating him to get his conscience right not to compare what he speaks to anybody's for he does not speak to anybody but God. In other words, most times out of ignorance and may be out of jealousy others turn to drift from their God-given gifts and talents or positions. These individuals allow the gifts and talents and positions of others to dictate the pace of their lives forgetting that we are different people with different gifting. The worst of all is when

God's people or believers want to be like or to live and do things like unbelievers whilst even unbelievers would not like to copy what believers do.

Key Quotation: 1 Samuel 8:1-9,

"When Samuel grew old, he appointed his sons as judges for Israel. The name of his firstborn was Joel and the name of the second was Abijah, and they served at Beersheba, But his sons did not walk in his ways. They turned aside after dishonest gain and accepted bribes and perverted justice. So, all the elders of Israel gathered together and came to Samuel at Ramah. They said to him, "You are old, and your sons do not walk in your ways; now appoint a king to lead us, such as all the nations have." But when they said "give us a king to lead us" this displeased Samuel; so he prayed the Lord. And the Lord told him "listen to all that the people are saying to you; its not you they have rejected, but they have rejected me as their king. As they have done from the day I brought them up out of Egypt until this day, forsaking me and serving other gods, so they are doing to you. Now listen to them, but warn them solemnly and let them know what the king who will reign over them will do."

Moses was the first leader of Israel, then Joshua and judges after Joshua. Samuel was the last judge and the bible says when he was old, he appointed his sons to judge Israel but because of their bad behaviour of accepting bribe the people rejected them and asked Samuel to give them a king instead for they wanted to be like the nations around them. In verse 6-9, both Samuel and God were upset with their request. God said to Samuel it's not you they reject but me. Why was God not upset with Samuel and his sons as he was with Eli and his sons? I believe God was not upset because they wanted a king and wanted to be like the nations around them which he had already warned them about. (Leviticus 20:26) In verse 9, God said to Samuel grant them their request but warn them of the consequences of rejecting my leadership for a king.

Vs. 10-17: the consequences of a king and fulfilments.

"Samuel told all the words of the Lord to the people who were asking him for a king. "This is what the king who will reign over you will do; He will take your sons and make them serve with his chariots and horses, and they will run in front of his chariots. Some he will assign to be commanders of thousands and commanders of fifties, and others to plow his ground and reap his harvest, and still others to make weapons of war and equipment for his chariots. He will take your daughters to be perfumers and cooks and bakers. He will take the best your fields and vineyards and olive groves and give them to his attendants. He will take a tenth of your grain and of your vintage and give it to his officials and attendants. Your menservants and maidservants and the best of your cattle and donkeys he will take for his own use. He will take a tenth of your flocks, and you yourselves will become his slaves."

Have you ever made a wrong decision or choice because you wanted to be like someone else? Like Israel, have you rejected or refused to work with what is in your hand, which is God's will in your life for something else? There is a consequence for that. Israel wanted a king because they wanted to be like the nations around them and they faced consequences as a result. Therefore I say be content with whatever the Lord has given you; don't compare yourself with anyone else for no one knows God's intentions for anyone. I also believe strongly that though sometimes out of ignorance we drift from God's will in our lives yet most times we do that out of jealousy – I want to have it not because I need it but because someone has got it.

Somebody jumps into marriage because someone has done it, someone wants to drive a car or live a luxury life not because God wants him to but because someone has it. We change our God-given Husbands, Wives, Jobs or Carriers – I will do it because someone has done it, even Churches and Church leaders. Some parents out of jealousy of others push their children to do what they are not called to do which ends up in disaster. The worst part of the matter is when believers want to be like unbelievers as I said earlier and dress, eat, drink and act like them. Can I advise my fellow workers in Christ who may be trying to be what they are not called to be, regardless of the unpopularity of your call, don't try to be like someone it is very dangerous. Prophets and those doing miracles may be popular, respected and even rich because of the nature of their call, don't force yourself, stay on course for what you've been called to be and remember that God gives grace and ability to everyone for whatever you've been called to be.

Finally in 1 Samuel 8:18, the Lord said:

"When that day comes, you will cry out for relief from the king you have chosen, and the LORD will not answer you in that day." (ANIV)

Never blame God for a consequence of your sin or mistake; cry to him in repentance. Many people when they face the consequences of their sin or mistake, they begin to apportion blame and pointing fingers on others even on God neglecting the fact that they are the cause of everything. I hope you have learnt lessons from the above story as I remind you that whatever happened to Israel or any other person can happen to you too if you fail to be content with what the Lord has put in your hand for God is no respecter of persons.

Your Availability Will Always Make You Special:

※

---

1 Samuel 16:14-23 speaks of David a shepherd boy for the sake of his gift as a harp player making his way into the palace of Saul under the King's invitation which led him to become one of his service men. Like David I have seen and heard of many men and women who have come from obscure places or positions to become icons, heroes, idols and celebrities and now rated among the well-known men and women of our time because of their gifts and talents. Some of these people did so because of the help of others who discovered the gifts in these individuals and therefore decided to help them operate in their gifts. As a result, these people are now enjoying the life they did not dream will ever happen to them. Some of these people are now well-known as top footballers, athletes, boxers and musicians today. To the glory of God I have come from an obscure background to be well known because of the gift of God in me, the

power to preach and teach the word of God to the understanding of all those who hear or listen to me. You can also do the same, even more if you realize what is in your hand and therefore begin to do something with it before you die and the gift or the talent becomes wasted. Solomon said,

> "Whatever your hand finds to do, do it with all your might, for in the grave, where you are going, there is neither working nor planning nor knowledge nor wisdom." Ecclesiastes 9:10 (ANIV)

It is sad sometimes that some people act like children and we deny God of what he has put in our hand forgetting that he gave us the power to become who we are as Moses told the Israelites.

> "And you shall remember the LORD your God, for *it is* He who gives you power to get wealth, that He may establish His covenant which He swore to your fathers, as *it is* this day." - Deuteronomy 8:18 (NKJV)

Never be like children who refuse to give to others or offer them food or sweets. Make available to God the little that you have, begin to trade with the seed in your hand, your gift or talent. I mean make an effort to do something with what is in your hand; it is the key to your future progress and the Lord will bring the increase as Paul said

"Now may He who supplies seed to the sower, and bread for food, supply and multiply the seed you have *sown* and increase the fruits of your righteousness,"
(2 Corinthians 9:10)

Like Moses, you only have to stretch your hand with what is in your hand and he who has the power will cause the wind to blow what will open the red sea of your life. God will always do his part if you will first do your part for all those who make available their gifts or talents or make use of what is in their hands will always receive increase but those who stay idle or do nothing with what they have even what they have will be taken away from them as Jesus told his disciples in the Parable of the Talents in Matthew 25:14-30,

"Again, it will be like a man going on a journey, who called his servants and entrusted his property to them. To one he gave five talents of money, to another two talents, and to another one talent, each according to his ability. Then he went on his journey. The man who had received the five talents went at once and put his money to work and gained five more. So also, the one with the two talents gained two more. But the man who had received the one talent went off, dug a hole in the ground and hid his master's money. "After a long time the master of those servants returned and settled accounts with them. The man who had received the five talents brought the other five. 'Master,' he said, 'you entrusted me with five talents. See, I have gained five more.' "His master replied, 'Well done, good and faithful servant! You have been faithful with a few things; I will put you in charge of many things. Come and share your master's happiness!' "The man with the two talents also came. 'Master,' he said, 'you entrusted me with two talents; see, I have gained two more.' "His master replied, 'Well done, good and faithful servant! You have been faithful with a few things; I will put you in charge of many things. Come and share your master's happiness!' "Then the man who had received the one talent came. 'Master,' he said, 'I knew that you are a hard man, harvesting where you have not sown and gathering where you have not scattered seed. So I was afraid and went out and hid your talent in the ground. See, here is what belongs to you.' "His master replied, 'You wicked, lazy servant! So you knew that I

harvest where I have not sown and gather where I have not scattered seed? Well then, you should have put my money on deposit with the bankers, so that when I returned I would have received it back with interest." 'Take the talent from him and give it to the one who has the ten talents. For everyone who has will be given more, and he will have an abundance. Whoever does not have, even what he has will be taken from him. And throw that worthless servant outside, into the darkness, where there will be weeping and gnashing of teeth."
- Matthew 25:14-30 (ANIV)

So what do you do? It is easier to say "It's all over, I am finished, I don't have enough, what I have is too small, I cannot do anything with it and so I have given up, but my advice to you is never write yourself off, and don't give up in what you have for the best is yet to come, try again and keep on trying, tomorrow could be your day. The little boy who says I will try will always make it into the hill top but the one who says I can't, I can't, will also always be under the hill. Just respect and work with what you have irrespective of how small it may be or insignificant it may look. Many have failed to work with what they have because they felt it is insignificant or small. In terms of marriage, the Lord told me when I was writing that someone's life has been turned upside down because he or she failed to recognise his/her spouse as the seed or the tool God has given him or her, the key to his/her prosperity or blessing. As you read this book or listen to me preach I pray that you see your wife or husband as your seed of success or what you have in your hand and begin to respect and work with her/him irrespective of their status or educational background and you will see your increase or blessing.

When the Lord gave me this message like most preachers little did I know the Lord was speaking to me also to do something with what I had in my hand, his calling in my life and by his grace and the leading of the Holy Spirit I have started trading with what is in my hand, that is, what the Lord has given me knowing that or being confident of this, that he who began a good work in me will carry it on to completion until the day of Christ Jesus. - Philippians 1:6 (ANIV) Like Paul I am fully persuaded that irrespective of how hard it is in the beginning, very soon my toil as a result of planting my seed or working with what is in my hand will pay dividends and I will enjoy the fruit of what I have done, sleepless night praying and waiting on the Lord for messages and praying to God to increase his anointing on me will begin to pay off. And I believe he will do the same for you if you will also follow his leading and work with what is in your hand.

The woman of Zarephath

Here is another person who did not withhold what she had from God but made it available and so reaped the result.

"Then the word of the Lord came to him, saying, "Arise, go to Zarephath, which belongs to Sidon, and dwell there. See, I have commanded a widow there to provide for you." So he arose and went to Zarephath. And when he came to the gate of the city, indeed a widow was there gathering sticks. And he called to her and said, "Please bring me a little water in a cup, that I may drink." And as she was going to get it, he called to her and said, "Please bring me a morsel of bread in your hand." So she said, "As the Lord your God lives, I do not have bread, only a handful of flour in a bin, and a little oil in a jar; and see, I am gathering a couple of sticks that I may go in and prepare it for myself and my son, that we may eat it, and die."And Elijah said to her, "Do not fear; go and do as you have said, but make me a small cake from it first, and bring it to me; and afterward make some for yourself and your son. For thus says the Lord God of Israel: 'The bin of flour shall not be used up, nor shall the jar of oil run dry, until the day the Lord sends rain on the earth.' So she went away and did according to the word of Elijah; and she and he and her household ate for many days. The bin of flour was not used up, nor did the jar of oil run dry, according to the word of the Lord which He spoke by Elijah."

(1 Kings 17:8-16)

Never hide from God or withhold from the Lord what you have or deny him but faithfully make available to him what you have and as I always say "your availability will always make you special." He has the power to increase what he has given you. He gave us an example of faithfulness in giving and the result when he gave us his only begotten son which has yielded millions of sons and daughters in the world today for him as a result. Making yourself or what you have, your gift, talent available is an investment in God which will always bring increase. Not like the poor singer who said "if I had a thousand tongues I will sing to praise my God for what he has done for me" for you will not be faithful in the big if you are not faithful in the small. Like people who want to get big money before they give to God in tithes and offerings. Begin to trade with the smaller that you have, give out of your small income or what you have and it will be easy to give when you have bigger.

I remember talking to Sonnie Badu a renowned Ghanaian music minister of God, Sonnie is an example of someone who is faithfully using what is in his hand to serve the Lord. He said to me one of the reasons why many of African gospel music and the musicians have been over shadowed and also why many people don't excel in their gift is that they don't add value to the gift. Sonnie advises that before anybody can excel in your gift you must add value to it. In my words I will say you must be thankful to God for the gift or talent and be willing to use it for the Lord's glory as Sonnie is doing when he holds microphone on platform he gives his all to praise God. If you serve God with this character God will surely bless you. I also remember after having this conversation with Minister Badu I sat my son down who is a keyboard and a drummer player in our church and said to him 'do you know that there are many keyboard and drummer players in this world so if he wants to make a difference he must add value to his skills and also do so with willingness of heart to serve God. I thank God for his life as I see that he has heeded to my advice and is doing very well for the Lord. I want to offer you this same advice as you read this book that use your gift or talent diligently and willingly, add value to whatever you do, look for ways to develop what you do, learn from others and you will be exceptional.

✷

Trust and Obey

Trusting and obeying the will of God will make the difference. The size and the location of what you have or what is in your hand does not matter; what matters is being in God's will for your life by believing God and using what he has given. Lot chose first the fertile and the best part of the land but Abraham had the promise of God, God's purpose for his life, so he prospered even though his part of the land was not as good as Lot's one (Genesis 13).

In Genesis 13:10-17, we read:

> "Lot looked up and saw that the whole plain of the Jordan was well watered, like the garden of the LORD, like the land of Egypt, towards Zoar. (This was before the LORD destroyed Sodom and Gomorrah.) So Lot chose for himself the whole plain of the Jordan and set out towards the east. The two men parted company: Abram lived in the land of Canaan, while Lot lived among the

cities of the plain and pitched his tents near Sodom. Now the men of Sodom were wicked and were sinning greatly against the LORD. The LORD said to Abram after Lot had parted from him, "Lift up your eyes from where you are and look north and south, east and west. All the land that you see I will give to you and your offspring for ever. I will make your offspring like the dust of the earth, so that if anyone could count the dust, then your offspring could be counted. Go, walk through the length and breadth of the land, for I am giving it to you." (ANIV)

From the above quotation, I therefore advice you not to waste your time measuring and thinking about what you can do with what you have because it is not the best one as others have trusted God's ability to succeed for God can use smaller things to achieve greater results. The bible says: He uses the weak things of this world to bring glory to himself. Paul said:

"Brothers, think of what you were when you were called. Not many of you were wise by human standards; not many were influential; not many were of noble birth. But God chose the foolish things of the world to shame the wise; God chose the weak things of the world to shame the strong. He chose the lowly things of this world and the despised things and the things that are not to nullify the things that are, so that no-one may boast before him." - 1 Corinthians 1:26-29 (ANIV)

You may feel that your ability, experience, or education makes you an unlikely candidate for God's service or nothing good can come out of you. Don't limit God's ability and don't limit yourself for all things are possible to them that believe. God can use you if you will only trust and obey him.

Peter and John

"Now Peter and John went up together to the temple at the hour of prayer, the ninth *hour*. And a certain man lame from his mother's womb was carried, whom they laid daily at the gate of the temple which is called Beautiful, to ask alms from those who entered the temple; who, seeing Peter and John about to go into the temple, asked for alms. And fixing his eyes on him, with John, Peter said, "Look at us." So he gave them his attention, expecting to receive something from them.

> Then Peter said, "Silver and gold I do not have, but what I do have I give you: In the name of Jesus Christ of Nazareth, rise up and walk." And he took him by the right hand and lifted *him* up, and immediately his feet and ankle bones received strength."
> (Acts 3:1-7)

We can see from the above Scripture that when Peter and John realized they have the name of Jesus and therefore used it, a great miracle followed which became one of the basis of the growth of the early church and a great demonstration of God's power that brought a lot of people to Christ. All believers will experience the power of God at work in us if we will recognise what we have at our disposal in terms of Jesus' name. Jesus said,

> "And these signs will follow those who believe: In My name they will cast out demons; they will speak with new tongues; they will take up serpents; and if they drink anything deadly, it will by no means hurt them; they will lay hands on the sick, and they will recover." - Mark 16:17-18 (NKJV)

Table Tennis Balls

A friend told me a story which I think will be relevant to this. He said, God commanded a minister to go and start a church in a city where he had no contact and knew no one. This minister apart from his ministerial job was also very good at table tennis and so when he was going he went with his table tennis kit. On his prayer list asking God how to start since he had no connection with anyone in the city the Lord asked him 'what is in your hand?' Your table tennis kit of course so he went and bought a table, set up his kits and very soon he had people with him all the time playing so as they played day after day he began sharing the word with them and very soon his playing mates became the foundation of the great work the Lord is doing through him in that city. Who knows that the Lord could be doing something through table tennis kits? You may also be asking how will I do it, how should I start? I will say just believe, just start with that little insignificant thing in your hand and God will fulfil his part; you are only an instrument.

Mary did not know how a virgin could get pregnant since she had known no man but God can do whatever he wants to do because all things are possible with him. Luke 1:34-38 says,

---

"How will this be," Mary asked the angel, "since I am a virgin?" The angel answered, "The Holy Spirit will come upon you, and the power of the Most High will overshadow you. So the holy one to be born will be called the Son of God. Even Elizabeth your relative is going to have a child in her old age, and she who was said to be barren is in her sixth month. For nothing is impossible with God." "I am the Lord's servant," Mary answered. "May it be to me as you have said." Then the angel left her." (ANIV)

If God could perform such a great miracle which a virgin conceiving without knowing any man, I promise you he can and will do the same for you if you will only trust and obey his word to you.

My Testimony

I thank the Lord after years of trying to be a business man after my education with my number one priority of becoming very rich in order to be able to support the work of God financially with the greatest of my heart desire was to be able to support ministers or pastors so that they could be able to do the work of God cheerfully and willingly. I have now come to know what the Lord has called me to do, his purpose for my life which I am now doing with diligence and willingness of heart as a preacher and a teacher of God's word and even now also as an author preaching and teaching the word of God through book writing, something I never dreamt of doing in my life. I want you to know that you will excel in doing what the Lord has called you to do than doing any other work in life as I said earlier on. My congregation and all those who listen to me preach and teach both in church and on radio will testify to this fact that I preach and teach with passion; in fact I love to preach and teach God's word. Sometimes people tell me and even I myself wonder where I get some of my words from when I am in my business of preaching or teaching. The secret is that I am in the will of God, His purpose for my life and I am using what is in my hand and so I am led by the Spirit of God whenever I am in business for the Lord. One of my members who is always listening to me almost all the time has repeatedly been telling me to stop saying sometimes when I am about to preach that I may not be able to preach long for a reason because he says even those days that I say that are even the days I preach with power and even long. He also says when I begin to preach it's like I become a different person and even sometimes I don't want to stop. Again I am currently preparing a guideline for preachers and teachers of God's Word as I am directed by the Spirit of God. Look for a copy if you are or desire to be a preacher or teacher of God's Word.

As I said earlier on, many people are struggling in life because they are not doing what they have been called to do or they are not using what is in their hand. Beginning to use what is in your hand, your seed like me might not be easy in the beginning but I can promise you there is a good time ahead, the season of harvest is on the way. Even I in my preaching, teaching and writing books am facing a lot of challenges but without doubt I know the harvest time is on the way. Therefore just be patient and carry on with the hope of a better future ahead. The farmer has the patience to wait for the day of harvest the very day he starts to till his land so he has the patience to wait. When James wrote to advice his readers to be patient as they wait for the coming of the lord he said:

"Therefore be patient, brethren, until the coming of the Lord. See how the farmer waits for the precious fruit of the earth, waiting patiently for it until it receives the early and latter rain." - James 5:7 (NKJV)

Read my book 'Be Ye Transformed' under my personal journey and you will see one of my embarrassing experiences that happened to me in my initial time of preaching but I did not give up till today I am happy to share it as an encouragement to others who would like to do something for the Lord. I can say to the glory of God that in my area and even beyond I have become a well known preacher and a teacher of God's word. Every time I go to a program and my name is mentioned people come to me later to say encouraging words like 'oh Pastor I am glad', some say 'I am blessed to see you here', 'God bless you for your messages that you preach on the radio' and so on.

✷

Aborted Seeds

Like many women who through abortion, an operation or other intervention to end a pregnancy by removing an embryo or foetus from the womb ending the life of an innocent child which many have regretted later, the reason why many are poor and broke today is that they have abandoned or aborted what is in their hand, God's purpose for their lives; they have neglected or thrown away their seed, gift or talent because of ignorance or due to the advice of others. The worst of all are those who like the stupid servant have also buried their gifts and talents. Others also have failed even though they are using what the Lord has given them because they proudly or wrongly misused it. Humbly use what the Lord has given you for he will always see to prosper what he has given for he will always be true to his word. The bible says:

"Likewise you younger people, submit yourselves to *your* elders. Yes, all of *you* be

> submissive to one another, and be clothed with humility, for *"God resists the proud, But gives grace to the humble. Therefore humble yourselves under the mighty hand of God, that He may exalt you in due time,"* (1 Peter 5:5-6)

Misusing what the Lord has given you will mean cheating others with your gift or talent and also using it in the wrong manner and in wrong places. I have lived in the United Kingdom for many years and have come across many people with exceptional gifts and talents but for the fact that these people are doing other jobs to earn their living having neglected their own gifts and talents life has become very difficult. Many of these people could not use what they have because of lack of proper documents, others needed quick money refusing to spend few months or even years to do refresher courses, the worse of all to me are those who are refusing to use what they have because of pride thinking that they are doing so to hurt somebody. Others also began very well with their seed but ended up badly because they digress from the Lord's way to their own way. King Saul is a typical example of this fact. He began very well under the will and direction of God but he ended up with the Lord rejecting him because he chose to do things in his own way and he lost his kingship as a result. 1 Samuel 15:22-23 says:

> "But Samuel replied: "Does the LORD delight in burnt offerings and sacrifices as much as in obeying the voice of the LORD? To obey is better than sacrifice, and to heed is better than the fat of rams. For rebellion is like the sin of divination, and arrogance like the evil of idolatry. Because you have rejected the word of the LORD, he has rejected you as king"

(ANIV). People may even laugh at you in the beginning but since it has been given to you by God, it will accomplish big things in your life for every big thing begins with a small seed. A small seed planted will become a big tree with abundance of fruits. Never let go of your seed, gift or talent, it may seem little like a cloud of a size of a man's hand in the days of Elijah but it is the beginning of a great rain, something big in your life as is recorded in 1 Kings 18:43-45,

> "And said to his servant, "Go up now, look toward the sea." So he went up and looked, and said, *"There is* nothing." And seven times he said, "Go again." Then it came to pass the seventh *time,* that he said, "There is a cloud, as small as a man's hand, rising out of the sea!" So he said, 'Go up, say to Ahab, 'Prepare *your chariot,* and go down before the rain stops you.'" Now it happened in the meantime that the sky became black with clouds and wind, and there was a heavy rain. So Ahab rode away and went to Jezreel." (NKJV)

CHILDREN ARE GIFTS FROM GOD

To some who may not know, I have come to announce to you that what you have in your hand is the children God has given you. What are you doing about them? The Psalmist said

> "Behold, children *are* a heritage from the LORD, The fruit of the womb *is* a reward" - Psalms 127:3 (NKJV)

When I was writing this book I had a dream one night and in the dream were so many people climbing very steep and long steps up and on my way I came up to a woman with two children who was very tired and finding it very difficult to climb because of the children in her hand so many people going past her. Realizing her problem I asked her: Where is your husband? With an angry and dejected voice she said 'he has left me only to care for the children.' Hearing that as we moved on I began to advice the woman by encouraging her not to give up and try to do everything she could to bring up the children for she will reap the result of her hard work in the future. I remember also in the dream I was telling the woman in the dream that what many don't know is that some children will also do the same to their parents who abandoned or refuse to take care of them when they were children. Suddenly I woke up and began to figure what could be the meaning of the dream and the Spirit of the Lord said, "Children are gifts from God" taking good care of your children, giving them good education and better training is giving good care to your seed and adding value to your gift.

I would like to advice all parents especially my fellow men under the direction of the Holy Spirit 'never abandon your child/children, never neglect them because if you do, you have abandoned or neglected your gift. Who knows that that child you are holding or neglecting is a future Prime Minister, a doctor an engineer or a minister of God's Word? Where I come from, I have seen many poor parents whose lives have been transformed because of the children they suffered and went through difficult times to bring up. Some of these parents are now living in better houses built for them by their children, others have been moved to live in the cities by their children, and some of these parents even have migrated to live or visited their children in other countries where their children are living; what a pride to any parent! But they deserve every bit of it because they have suffered for it. Someone said his children are his investment and that he will do everything to bring them up very well so that when he retires he will enjoy the fruit of his labour. Like this man I advise you that among many other things also invest in your children and it will help you in the future. Many parents' investments are clothes and what they will enjoy themselves today which does not yield any dividends in the future.

Again I say never be like the father of those children I saw in the dream, don't run from your responsibility as parents; rather face it, it's a blessing. You may not have gone to school nor had the chance to learn any trade may be as a result of your parents but please never pass that on to your children; determine to help your children go beyond your level to become what you failed to become. They are your gift from God, they *are* a heritage from the LORD, and they are your future in your hand in this context. Don't say as some parents said and have paid the price for what they said that "after all I did not have the opportunity to go to school or be highly educated; why should my children? I think this is primitive and wicked as a parent. I thank God for my parents especially my mother who is still alive for her hard work to bring me to the level I am now and like every child I will forever be indebted to her so long as she is alive. May God bless her with long life to benefit from her hard work having raised eight children, four boys and four girls.

You are responsible for your child/children. Paul said:

"Now I am ready to visit you for the third time, and I will not be a burden to you, because what I want is not your possessions but you. After all, children should not have to save up for their parents, but parents for their children." 2 Corinthians 12:14 (NIV 2011)

I would also take this opportunity to advise everybody, adult or a child since we were all given birth to by someone, never forget your parents, see to it that you will also pay them back for what they have done for you and God will bless you.

Paul wrote to his son in God Timothy. He said

"But if any widow has children or grandchildren, let them first learn to show piety at home and to repay their parents; for this is good and acceptable before God".
1 Tim 5:4 (NKJV)

Conclusion

What is in your hand? What do you see as something the Lord has given you? In the kingdom of God and in your personal life, what do you see as your gift or talent God has given you or what do you see as your tool? What you see as so small in your life is just a seed; it is the key to your greatness in the future. Think about it!

Until you realize what you have and begin to do something with it, you will always be crying for your means to live while you are sitting on a pot of gold, because, a seed will remain single until it is planted and given a chance to multiply. No one is a wasted item in the kingdom of God or in God's hand. God can use anything or anybody to produce something great. The Scripture says:

"For we are His workmanship, created in Christ
Jesus for good works, which God prepared

beforehand that we should walk in them."
(Ephesians 2:10)

Begin to do something now for a Ghanaian proverb says: 'When you stay in one place you may be sitting on your inheritance.' This means don't be lazy, don't hang unto just one thing or one place; move on.

In the kingdom of God, what do you see in your hand or what do you see as your seed? What gift or talent do you have? Don't look down upon yourself or allow anyone to look down on you. Never say I am good for nothing or I don't have anything, neither say I can't do it; it's not who you are or what you can do but who he (God) is and what he (God) can do through you. Just make the little that you have available to him and he will bring the increase.

Consider yourself as God's workmanship (work of art, masterpiece) a child of God who is able to do all things through Christ as Paul said

---

"I can do all things through Christ who strengthens me." Philippians 4:13 (NKJV)

Conclusion

With the shepherd's rod of Moses, God did great miracles but not until Moses had added value to the rod (what he had in his hand). With what was in his hand Moses performed one of the greatest miracles recorded in Scripture by opening the red sea for the Israelites to cross on dry land.

"And the LORD said to Moses, "Why do you cry to Me? Tell the children of Israel to go forward. But lift up your rod, and stretch out your hand over the sea and divide it. And the children of Israel shall go on dry *ground* through the midst of the sea." (Exodus 14:15-16)

"Then Moses stretched out his hand over the sea; and the LORD caused the sea to go *back* by a strong east wind all that night, and made the sea into dry *land,* and the waters were divided. So the children of Israel went into the midst of the sea on the dry *ground,* and the waters *were* a wall to them on their right hand and on their left."
(Exodus 14:21-22)

I want you to understand as I believe this is what the Lord was telling Moses that as much as it is good to pray, there are at times when God expects us to back our prayers with action. I believe the Lord was telling Moses there is a time for everything, stop crying and do something now with what is in your hand. Many Christians have prayed for years and are still praying instead of taking a bold step in the situation they are using prayer as an excuse and are praying every day, waiting for God to drop Manna from heaven. I want you to know that the time of Manna is over; if you are praying for a job, make an effort in looking for a job. Again I declare to you that "It is time for action" time to move on.

As we have already learnt, you should go to God in prayer to ask him what he has given as a talent, ability or your seed if you are still struggling to know what you have. Also I have asked you to examine your life to see what you find easy to do. I will also say be sure of the inner testimony of what you think the Lord is telling you for the enemy who is always an impostor can bring something to you when you request from God to show you what he has given you. Take a bold step to begin to use what you have irrespective of how or where you are beginning and the increase will come from the Lord. Most often, it could be a risk but don't panic and don't give up for if God gives you a vision he will also give you the provision. Just like a pregnancy, your part of the process is taking good care of yourself and the growth is God's part. If God could do a miracle through four lepers who risked their lives in taking a bold courageous step to bring food to starving people of Samaria, he could do the same for you. - 2 Kings 7:3-9 (ANIV)

Like the lepers, why do you stay idle with your talent and suffer? Start to do something and the Lord will cause your faith to open up doors for you. Also always remember to give God the glory for your success and always acknowledge him to be number one in all that you do.

Also remember:

- The poor widow's oil multiplied when she made it available
- With the 17 year old boy's single stone out of 5 he killed a giant

- With 2 fish and five bread of a young boy, Jesus fed 5,000 men without women and children counted
- Peter and John healed a cripple with the name of Jesus Christ

You can also be doing exploits with the little you have if you will recognise what you have and begin to use it; that is by adding value to what you have and begin to do something with it irrespective of the size or how insignificant it may seem in your eyes or in the eyes of others. Notice that it is the Lord who gives the increase. Notice also that having no confidence in yourself or self-disbelieve due to fear and unbelief and inferiority complex and others will always quench and prevent you from seeing what is in your hand but faith in God will release who you are and what you have; it will also always put you on top. You may be doing something which could not be what you have been called to do. Prayerfully look at what you are doing to avoid time-wasting.

Israel wanted a king like other nations around them and they suffered as a result because the Lord was angry with them. You may want to leave your husband/wife to lead a single life because your friend is doing it, you may want a tall, fat, rich, brown or white man or woman, but be careful. There are consequences to taking what is not meant for you. What have you forsaken or refused to accept which was to be your God-given thing, (what is in your hand in the context of this book) and have suffered the consequence? Be mindful of any decision you make; you may be forsaking what God meant for you, you may be refusing what God has put in your hand. The worst of all is when you want to do it because of what others are doing or saying and when you as a Christian are trying to live and do things like unbelievers whilst unbelievers on the other hand even hate to be like believers. Believers are meant to be the salt and the light of the world. Don't compare yourself to anyone to do things because someone has done what he or she is doing; it may not be meant for you so don't rush in life. Be grateful to God for whatever he has put in your hand for He knows best.

What is the state of your children? What foundation are you giving to your children knowing that life is like the foundation of a building which is very critical, the stronger of the foundation of a building, the stronger the whole building. Are you sure the foundation you are giving your children can withstand the storm of life in this evil world we live in? Think about this! Always remember that: Your children are a heritage from the Lord, your gift and your future. Looking after them without abandoning them is fulfilling the responsibility the Lord has given you which will bring blessings to you in the future. Who knows what that child is going to be in the future; so abandoning your child is abandoning your future.

Again and finally I ask you: **"What is in your hand?"** It is the key to your future progress, use it! I believe your days or hours of reading this book has not been in vain but will help you to realize what you have in your hand. Always remember you have your future in your hand!

God bless you!

✼

Other Books By The Author

Pastor David Amoah –

- Lead Us Not Into Temptation
- Be Ye Transformed
- Stay Connected To Christ – Coming soon

www.ingramcontent.com/pod-product-compliance
Lightning Source LLC
Chambersburg PA
CBHW071455080526
44587CB00014B/2115